# BRAZIL IN A NUTSHELL

# AN ESSENTIAL GUIDE AND PHRASEBOOK FOR TRAVELERS

# BRAZIL IN A NUTSHELL

**MARK G. NASH**
**WILLIANS RAMOS FERREIRA**

© 2012 Mark G. Nash & Willians Ramos Ferreira
Preparação de texto: Juliane Kaori / Verba Editorial
Capa e Projeto gráfico: Alberto Mateus
Diagramação: Crayon Editorial
Assistente editorial: Aline Naomi Sassaki

**Dados Internacionais de Catalogação na Publicação (CIP)**
**(Câmara Brasileira do Livro, SP, Brasil)**

Nash, Mark G.
  Brazil in a nutshell : an essential guide and phrasebook for travelers / Mark G. Nash, Willians Ramos Ferreira. – Barueri, SP : DISAL, 2012.

  ISBN 978-85-7844-092-3

  1. Conversação 2. Inglês – Vocabulários e manuais de conversação I. Ferreira, Willians Ramos. II. Título.

11-11697                                              CDD-428.2469

**Índices para catálogo sistemático:**
1. Guia de conversação : Inglês : Linguística 428.2469
2. Inglês : Guia de conversação : Linguística 428.2469

Todos os direitos reservados em nome de:
Bantim, Canato e Guazzelli Editora Ltda.

Alameda Mamoré 911 – cj. 107
Alphaville – BARUERI – SP
CEP: 06454-040
Tel. / Fax: (11) 4195-2811
Visite nosso site: www.disaleditora.com.br
Televendas: (11) 3226-3111

Fax gratuito: 0800 7707 105/106
E-mail para pedidos: comercialdisal@disal.com.br

*Nenhuma parte desta publicação pode ser reproduzida, arquivada ou transmitida de nenhuma forma ou meio sem permissão expressa e por escrito da Editora.*

# Contents

About this book . . . . . . . . . . . . . . . . . . . . . . . . . . . . . . . . . . . . . . . . . . 7

**PART 1**   THE COUNTRY AND THE PEOPLE

Brazil at a glance . . . . . . . . . . . . . . . . . . . . . . . . . . . . . . . . . . . . . . . . 10

About Brazil  . . . . . . . . . . . . . . . . . . . . . . . . . . . . . . . . . . . . . . . . . . . 14

Climate and clothing tips. . . . . . . . . . . . . . . . . . . . . . . . . . . . . . . . . . 19

What to do and see in four of Brazil's most interesting urban centers . . 26

Food and drink  . . . . . . . . . . . . . . . . . . . . . . . . . . . . . . . . . . . . . . . . . 34

Health . . . . . . . . . . . . . . . . . . . . . . . . . . . . . . . . . . . . . . . . . . . . . . . . 45

Holidays and special dates in Brazil. . . . . . . . . . . . . . . . . . . . . . . . . . 48

Money matters. . . . . . . . . . . . . . . . . . . . . . . . . . . . . . . . . . . . . . . . . . 55

Crime and security in Brazil . . . . . . . . . . . . . . . . . . . . . . . . . . . . . . . 58

**PART 2**   COMMUNICATING IN BRAZIL

Survival language  . . . . . . . . . . . . . . . . . . . . . . . . . . . . . . . . . . . . . . . 62

Transportation. . . . . . . . . . . . . . . . . . . . . . . . . . . . . . . . . . . . . . . . . . 65

Money matters and shopping  . . . . . . . . . . . . . . . . . . . . . . . . . . . . . . 72

At the hotel  . . . . . . . . . . . . . . . . . . . . . . . . . . . . . . . . . . . . . . . . . . . . 75

On the telephone. . . . . . . . . . . . . . . . . . . . . . . . . . . . . . . . . . . . . . . . 78

Health issues and pharmacy  . . . . . . . . . . . . . . . . . . . . . . . . . . . . . . . 82

Food and eating out. . . . . . . . . . . . . . . . . . . . . . . . . . . . . . . . . . . . . . 86

Going out and dating. . . . . . . . . . . . . . . . . . . . . . . . . . . . . . . . . . . . . 96

Football / soccer. . . . . . . . . . . . . . . . . . . . . . . . . . . . . . . . . . . . . . . . 100

Olympic Games. . . . . . . . . . . . . . . . . . . . . . . . . . . . . . . . . . . . . . . . 104

Glossary of useful language . . . . . . . . . . . . . . . . . . . . . . . . . . . . . . . 114

## APPENDIX

Brazilian Portuguese pronunciation. . . . . . . . . . . . . . . . . . . . . . . . . 128

Useful phone numbers and websites . . . . . . . . . . . . . . . . . . . . . . . . . 134

# About this book

THE INTERNET AND search engines like Google have rendered the old-fashioned "tourist guide" almost obsolete. It has never been easier to get information about a country as it is today. We can research and book hotels and flights, rent cars and plan itineraries over the internet long before we leave our home country. Furthermore, with the availability of internet all over the world, and even in the remotest places, we can continually update and change our itinerary during the trip. This guide doesn't attempt to include information about places to visit or hotels or bus schedules. Our idea is to provide essential information about the country, a few pointers and tips and, more importantly, an essential glossary and phrasebook to communicate in Portuguese while you are in Brazil.

Travelers in foreign countries are often at a loss for words when confronted by daily situations of interaction. This guide will get you through most daily interactions in Portuguese. The phrasebook includes sections on what to say at the hotel, restaurant, on the phone, at the sports stadium, in a taxi and even how to flirt with people you meet at a night spot.

## How to use this book

The first part of the book provides essential information about the country and the people as well as useful information that every traveler needs to know. This section touches on issues like health, security, cuisine, tipping, electricity standards and other topics. Each topic is followed by a short glossary of related vocabulary words.

The second part of the book focuses on communicating in Brazil. It is composed of bilingual glossaries and phrases, organized by topic and location (at the hotel, at the restaurant, money issues, at the stadium etc.). It includes "survival phrases" that you will need to know and use during your stay in Brazil. These survival phrases include basics like "please" and "thank you" and other essential phrases like "Where is the bathroom?" and "How much is it?" The pronunciation appendix will help you with the pronunciation of the phrases. As a last resort, if your interlocutor doesn't understand what you're saying, you can always show them the phrase written in this guide, but we believe you'll have more fun speaking the phrases yourself.

A final note: we have kept the guide as small as possible so that it actually does fit in your pocket. After all, what's the point in having a big bulky guidebook if you end up leaving it back at the hotel rather than lug it around? Take this guide with you and enjoy your first steps in communicating in Portuguese. You'll have richer experiences in Brazil for it.

Boa viagem!

**PART 1**

# The country and the people

# Brazil at a glance

**NAME**
Federative Republic of Brazil (República Federativa do Brasil)

**CAPITAL**
Brasília

**LANGUAGES**
Portuguese (official), indigenous languages and some German and Italian in the south

**POPULATION**
190,732,694 (2010 census)

**GROSS DOMESTIC PRODUCT (GDP)**
R$ 3.675 trillion / US$ 2.1 trillion (2010)

**PER CAPITA INCOME (PCI)**
US$ 10,814 (2010)

BRAZIL AT A GLANCE

# The states of Brazil
(and state abbreviation) and their capitals

Acre • **AC** • Rio Branco
Alagoas • **AL** • Maceió
Amapá • **AP** • Macapá
Amazonas • **AM** • Manaus
Bahia • **BA** • Salvador
Ceará • **CE** • Fortaleza
Distrito Federal • **DF** • Brasília
Espírito Santo • **ES** • Vitória
Goiás • **GO** • Goiânia
Maranhão • **MA** • São Luís
Mato Grosso • **MT** • Cuiabá
Mato Grosso do Sul • **MS** • Campo Grande
Minas Gerais • **MG** • Belo Horizonte
Pará • **PA** • Belém
Paraíba • **PB** • João Pessoa
Paraná • **PR** • Curitiba
Pernambuco • **PE** • Recife
Piauí • **PI** • Teresina
Rio de Janeiro • **RJ** • Rio de Janeiro
Rio Grande do Norte • **RN** • Natal
Rio Grande do Sul • **RS** • Porto Alegre
Rondônia • **RO** • Porto Velho
Roraima • **RR** • Boa Vista
Santa Catarina • **SC** • Florianópolis
São Paulo • **SP** • São Paulo
Sergipe • **SE** • Aracaju
Tocantins • **TO** • Palmas

BRAZIL AT A GLANCE

## Working hours

Working hours are usually from 8 a.m. or 9 a.m. to 5 p.m. or 6 p.m. Banks open Monday to Friday, from 10 a.m. to 4 p.m. In cities, shops are open from 9 a.m. to 6 p.m. or later. Shopping centers are open seven days a week from 10 a.m. to 10 p.m., or later if there is a movie theater. In small towns many shops close at noon on Saturday and only re-open on Monday. It is usually possible to find 24-hour convenience stores and pharmacies, even in small towns.

## Electricity

Brazil uses both 110 and 220 volts for everyday appliances, depending on the place. Outlets are usually not marked for voltage so ask before plugging in. Recently, Brazil adopted a new three-prong plug and socket standard that, unfortunately, is not used by the rest of the world. Prior to this, Brazil used both the round two-prong European and flat two-prong and three-prong American plugs. Today you can find any one of these three options in use. Luckily, you can buy plug adapters at hardware stores and supermarkets.

### Key words

110 volts: **cento e dez volts**
220 volts: **duzentos e vinte volts**
capital: **capital**
city: **cidade**
language: **língua, idioma**
movie theater: **cinema**
plug adapter: **benjamin, adaptador**
plug: **plugue**
shopping center: **shopping**
socket: **tomada**
state: **estado**
store: **loja**

# About Brazil

**The land**

Look at a map of South America and you'll see that Brazil dominates the continent. It is by far the largest country in Latin America and the 5$^{th}$ largest in the world, covering an area of 8,514,877 square kilometers (3,287,597 square

The Amazon, the world's largest tropical forest

miles). It shares a common border with all countries in South America except Chile and Ecuador. No matter how you look at Brazil, it's large. Brazil is the 8$^{th}$ largest economy in the world. From north to south, its coastline is 7,491 kilometers long (4,655 miles). Brazil is home to the Amazon river, the second longest river in the world and the largest in volume of water. The Amazon discharges more fresh water into the ocean than the next ten largest rivers in the world combined. The vast interior plateau is one of the great breadbaskets of the world, producing soybeans, corn and other food crops. Brazil is the world's second largest producer of soybeans and has the largest herd of beef cattle on the planet. It supplies the bulk of coffee consumed around the world. The diverse climate of Brazil ranges from the cool mountains and plains of the south to the steaming humid tropics of the north. There are semi-arid savannas and rainforests, high mountains and plains, grasslands and jungle. In short, whatever you're looking for, you'll find it in Brazil. Brazilians are ever eager to point out that it even snows in the mountains in the south!

## The people

You'll also find diversity among the people, something inevitable in a country so large and made up of such different geographical regions. The only Portuguese-speaking country in Latin America doesn't speak just one Portuguese. The language and accents change as one travels from north to south and east to west. Then there are the 180 or so indigenous languages spoken in Brazil among the almost 500,000 Native Americans. The different immigrant groups

Multi-ethnic Brazil

that make up Brazil are not distributed equally geographically. There is the strong African influence in Bahia and parts of the northeast, the mix of European and Native American in the north and the Amazon, the multi-ethnic southeast, home to cities like São Paulo, made up of Italian, Portuguese, Japanese, Lebanese, Chinese and Syrian immigrants. Further south, the Italians, Germans, Poles and Ukrainians settled in the temperate mountains and to this day you can hear German spoken in some of the smaller towns.

In spite of all the diversity in Brazil, you'll find Brazilians have one thing in common: a warm heart. Visitors are made to feel welcome and you'll find the people are genuinely interested in meeting foreigners and learning about where they're from. Everywhere you go, you'll encounter acts of kindness from strangers.

## The economy

Fifteen years of economic stability, low inflation and a stable and strong currency have paid off for Brazil. Young Brazilians today enjoy a world their parents didn't know and only hoped for. No more hyperinflation, radical and often disastrous economic plans and foreign debt. Brazilians are consuming as never before and the economy is booming. Brazilian industry is investing and scrambling to keep pace with the rising demand for consumer goods. Brazil's role as a commodity giant is recognized the world over. Vale do Rio Doce, the Brazilian steel and mineral company, is the largest producer of iron ore in the world. Brazil has massive reserves of bauxite (aluminum) and ranks among the largest exporters of grains and food in the world. Brazil's oil reserves continue to grow in leaps and bounds as they continually discover massive new offshore deposits, like the recently discovered giant offshore "pre-salt" deposits. Brazil continues to climb in the ranking of known oil reserves and its national oil company, Petrobras, ranks among the biggest oil companies in the world and is the world leader in deep offshore drilling. In fact, the only significant new oil reserves discovered in the last decades have been in Brazil. The result of all this new wealth and development has been optimism.

The largest herd of beef cattle on the planet

Brazilians are proud of their new wealth and their important new role in the international scene. There is a feeling that Brazil's time has finally come and there's nothing that can stop this great country.

There are also problems to overcome in Brazil. Brazil continues to rank among the worst in Latin America in distribution of wealth. The country also has one of the highest tax burdens in the world and an expensive state bureaucracy to support. Much of the wealth is concentrated in few hands and regions, like the prosperous industrial southeast and the rich agricultural zones of Mato Grosso, the south and the high central plateau. The poorer north and northeast, in spite of recent growth and development, still lag behind in income, health, education and opportunity. Another problem that Brazil has to overcome — and one that affects visitors — is the high crime rate. These are just some of the challenges Brazilians will have to face in the next decades.

## Key words

beach: **praia**
border: **fronteira**
Brazilian: **brasileiro, brasileira**
coast: **costa**
country: **país**
economy: **economia**
forest: **mata, floresta**
kilometer: **quilômetro**
mountain range: **serra**
mountain: **montanha**
nation: **nação**
ocean: **oceano**
oil: **petróleo**
people: **população, povo**
region: **região**
river: **rio**
sea: **mar**
South America: **América do Sul**

BRAZIL IN A NUTSHELL

# Climate and clothing tips

BRAZIL CAN BE divided into five regions (see page 12), each in a different climatic zone, ranging from temperate in the mountains of the south and southeast to subtropical and humid tropical in the north. Most of the landmass in Brazil is tropical.

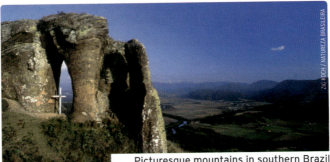
Picturesque mountains in southern Brazil

## The South region

The South region of Brazil is composed of the states of Rio Grande do Sul, Santa Catarina and Paraná. It enjoys cool winters with lows at night that can go below zero. Summer temperatures are warm, but often cool at night, especially in the mountains. Rainfall is distributed fairly evenly throughout the year. The cold fronts that come up from Argentina in the winter can bring cold drizzly days followed by cool, dry weather. Summer rain is typically the afternoon thundershowers of tropical climates.

**CLOTHING TIPS** Bring adequate warm clothes for the winter months.

## In the South region
### Don't miss ...

1 » The majestic Iguaçu falls and national park, Paraná
2 » The charming villages and beaches of Florianopolis, Santa Catarina
3 » The wine region of Bento Gonçalves, Rio Grande do Sul
4 » The Jesuit-Guarani mission ruins at São Miguel das Missões, Rio Grande do Sul
5 » The picturesque mountains and villages of the "Serra Catarinense", Santa Catarina

## The Southeast region

The Southeast region is composed of the states of São Paulo, Rio de Janeiro, Espírito Santo and Minas Gerais. This region, which straddles the Tropic of Capricorn, enjoys a subtropical to temperate climate. More than anything else, altitude determines the temperatures in the southeast. Cities like São Paulo (SP), São José dos Campos (SP) or Petrópolis (RJ), situated at 600 meters (1,980 feet) or more, have a cooler winter and summer nights are pleasant. Rio de Janeiro (RJ), Santos (SP) and the beach towns on the coast are cooler

The beautiful beaches of Rio de Janeiro

in the winter, but nothing like the near-zero temperatures that can occur in the mountains. Summer temperatures are high, averaging more than 30° C (86° F) and tropical thunderstorms are common at the end of the afternoon. The rainy season coincides with the summer months from December to March. Rainfall in the winter is usually limited to lighter, cool rain or drizzle brought with the cold fronts that come up from the south. Winter temperatures in the mountains can go down to 0° C (32° F) at night, but usually the night temperatures are pleasantly cool and in the 12° C to 20° C range (54° F to 68° F). Days are pleasant and warm for the most part.

**CLOTHING TIPS** Regular summer clothes are fine for the daytime, but if traveling in the southeast in winter, bring some fleece sweaters and a good rain jacket. You might want to pack something smart for going out in cosmopolitan São Paulo and Rio at night, where dress is more formal and fashionable.

## In the Southeast region
### Don't miss ...

1 » The beautiful city of Rio de Janeiro

2 » The colonial towns of Ouro Preto and Tiradentes in Minas Gerais

3 » The modern metropolis of São Paulo

4 » The beaches and hiking on Ilha Grande island, Rio de Janeiro

5 » The charming colonial coastal town of Parati, Rio de Janeiro

## The Central-West region

The Central-West region is composed of the states of Goiás, Mato Grosso, Mato Grosso do Sul and the Distrito Federal (Federal District), where the nation's capital, Brasília, is situated. A high plateau makes up part of the

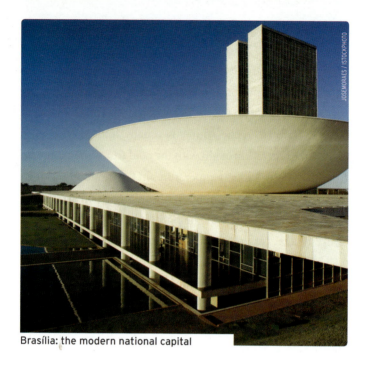
Brasília: the modern national capital

Central-West region. This plateau is a semi-arid savannah for the most part, although there is enough regular summer rainfall to support large-scale agriculture. The summers are hot and almost all the yearly rainfall occurs in this season (from October to March). Winters are dry and temperatures can drop to freezing at night. Much of the region is at 1,000 meters (3,300 feet) and has a pleasant, dry winter with cool nighttime temperatures. The region also contains the low-lying wetlands of the Pantanal with its characteristic humid tropical climate. Summers in the Pantanal are hot and rainfall abundant.

**CLOTHING TIPS:** You would be wise to bring breathable lightweight rain gear if you travel in the region in summer and some warm clothes to use on the high plateau in winter.

CLIMATE AND CLOTHING TIPS

### In the Central-West region
**Don't miss ...**

| | |
|---|---|
| 1 » | The Pantanal wetlands of Mato Grosso and its incredible wildlife |
| 2 » | The natural springs in Bonito, Mato Grosso |
| 3 » | The colonial town of Pirenópolis, Goiás |
| 4 » | The fantastic waterfalls and canyons in the Chapada dos Veadeiros national park, Goiás |
| 5 » | Brasília and its fascinating modern architecture |

## The Northeast region

The Northeast region is composed of the states of Maranhão, Piauí, Ceará, Rio Grande do Norte, Paraíba, Pernambuco, Alagoas, Sergipe and Bahia. Most of the cities are located on the coast or in the "zona da mata", the green agricultural belt that straddles the coast. In the northeast, as one moves inland from the coast the climate becomes drier and droughts are common further inland in the semi-arid

Coconut groves and white sand beaches in the northeast

"sertão". The climate is tropical with abundant sunshine year round. Temperatures on the coast are pleasant and tempered by constant trade winds. Temperatures average between 20° C and 28° C (68° F and 82° F), but in the high plateau inland it can be considerably cooler in the winter.

### In the Northeast region
#### Don't miss ...

1 » The colonial city of Olinda, Pernambuco
2 » The sand dunes and lagoons of Lençóis maranhenses, Maranhão
3 » The island and marine park of Fernando de Noronha, Pernambuco
4 » Jericoacoara beach, Ceará
5 » Salvador, Bahia and its rich Afro-Brazilian culture

The Amazon jungle is home to an astonishing biodiversity

CLIMATE AND CLOTHING TIPS

## The North region

The North region is composed of the states of Acre, Amazonas, Roraima, Rondônia, Pará, Amapá and Tocantins. This region, dominated by the Amazon river and basin, can be characterized as humid tropical. Rainfall is abundant and temperatures fairly constant year round averaging above 25º C (77º F).

**CLOTHING TIPS:** Aside from regular warm-weather clothes, bring breathable lightweight rain gear and waterproof hiking boots if planning on hiking in the jungle.

### In the North region
#### Don't miss ...

1 » The famous "encontro das águas" where the waters of the Negro and Solimões rivers meet, Amazonas

2 » The exotic Amazonian fruit, produce and fish at the municipal market in Manaus, Amazonas

3 » A trip into the Amazon forest to see some of the incredible biodiversity of the world's largest tropical forest

4 » The exotic port of Belém, Pará, at the mouth of the Amazon river

5 » The crystal-clear waters and wilderness of the Jalapão state park, Tocantins

### Key words

cold: **frio**
dry region inland in the northeast region: **sertão**
hot: **quente**
humid coastal belt in the northeast region: **zona da mata**
rain: **chuva**
summer: **verão**
sun: **sol**
winter: **inverno**

# What to do and see in four of Brazil's most interesting urban centers

IF ONE HAD to choose four cities to visit in Brazil, these would be excellent choices. A visit to the vibrant and sophisticated metropolis of São Paulo offers the chance to see the industrial, financial and cultural heart of the country. Rio offers plenty of natural beauty and charm as well as some of Brazil's most beautiful beaches. Brazil's African heritage is concentrated in Salvador, along with some of the richest colonial architecture in the country. Brasília, the planned city inaugurated in 1960 as the nation's new capital, is a "must-see" for its incredibly bold modern architecture and urban planning.

## 10 things to do and see in São Paulo

1 MASP (Museu de Arte de São Paulo) and Pinacoteca museums (Estação Pinacoteca). No visit to São Paulo would be complete without a visit to these two great museums.

## MOST INTERESTING URBAN CENTERS

**2** The Soccer Museum (Museu do futebol). This new museum is a must for soccer fans.

**3** Municipal Market (Mercado Municipal). If you enjoy food and the hustle and bustle of markets, you'll love the municipal market of São Paulo.

Cheese, olives and salami at the municipal market

**4** Ibirapuera park (Parque Ibirapuera). São Paulo's largest urban park is also where Paulistanos go to jog, walk, ride a bicycle, have a picnic beside the lake or just enjoy a bit of peace and quiet. The park is host to a number of excellent museums and exhibition centers.

**5** Butantan Institute (Instituto Butantan). Check out the large collection of snakes, spiders and other poisonous creatures and see the roughly 1,000 poisonous snakes being "milked" to make snake bite antidotes.

**6** Jardins. This dynamic and sophisticated neighborhood is the fashion center of São Paulo.

BRAZIL IN A NUTSHELL

**7** Liberdade. The most Japanese neighborhood in São Paulo. You can spend a very pleasant afternoon strolling around the streets of Liberdade enjoying the Japanese atmosphere, shops and restaurants.

**8** Municipal theater (Teatro Municipal) and the Sala São Paulo theater. If you have the chance, take in a concert or opera at either of these great theaters.

**9** Nightlife in Vila Madalena and Vila Olímpia. These two neighborhoods are known as the nightlife hotspots in São Paulo.

**10** Shopping on 25 de Março. Enjoy the shopping mayhem on the busiest shopping street in Latin America.

## 10 things to do and see in Rio

**1** Sugarloaf and cable car. The Pão de Açucar (Sugarloaf) and "bonde" (cable car) are probably the most-visited tourist attractions of Rio, and for good reason.

**2** Corcovado and the Cristo Redentor statue. This veritable symbol of Rio is another tourist attraction that can't be missed during your stay in Rio. Give yourself plenty of time to enjoy the views from the top.

The "Cristo Redentor" statue

## MOST INTERESTING URBAN CENTERS

**3** Cycle the waterfront of Zona Sul and Lagoa Rodrigo de Freitas. A great way to see Rio's most famous beaches is to rent a bicycle and explore the vibrant waterfront from Copacabana to Ipanema and then go around the Lagoa Rodrigo de Freitas lake.

**4** Botecos in Ipanema. No visit to Rio would be complete without a night out and a meal at one of Rio's famous informal "Botecos".

**5** Posto 9 and posto 10 at Ipanema beach. Nothing could be more "carioca" than Ipanema beach. The beach in front of lifeguard stations 9 and 10 is a great place to watch people or socialize and join in one of the impromptu beach volleyball or soccer games.

**6** Surf at Prainha and Grumari beaches. Two of Rio's most beautiful and pristine beaches. Prainha is the surfing hotspot for young people.

**7** Hang glide from Pedra Bonita. Magnificent views of the city and a great adrenaline rush for the more adventurous.

**8** Botanical gardens. One of the oldest and most beautiful botanical gardens in the world. It has an excellent collection of tropical species.

**9** Floresta da Tijuca. The Tijuca forest is the largest urban forest in the world and offers exceptional hiking, views and a chance to see tropical flora and fauna up close.

**10** The Rua General Glicério street fair in Laranjeiras. Every Saturday there are free street concerts where you can listen to authentic "chorinho".

## 10 things to do and see in Brasília

**1** Praça dos Três Poderes. One of the most interesting architectural complexes in Brazil and the seat of the country's three highest authorities: Congress, the Presidential Palace (Palácio do Planalto) and the Supreme Court.

**2** Palacio Itamaraty. This impressive building, designed by Oscar Niemeyer, houses the Ministry of Foreign Affairs.

**3** Catedral Metropolitana de Brasília. The Cathedral, with its 16 massive curved concrete pillars, is one of the world's most amazing modernist buildings.

The very modern "Catedral Metropolitana"

## MOST INTERESTING URBAN CENTERS

**4** Torre de TV. The TV tower, with its lookout deck, is a great place to watch the sunset and enjoy a panoramic view of the city.

**5** Palácio da Alvorada. This magnificent Niemeyer building is the official presidential residence and icon of Brasília.

**6** Jardim Botânico de Brasília. The botanical garden, spread over more than 5,000 hectares, is a great place to learn about the fauna and flora of the "Cerrado" region.

**7** Lago Paranoá. This urban artificial lake offers restaurants, parks, walking and bike paths and boat rides.

**8** Pirenópolis. This charming colonial town outside Brasília is well worth visiting.

**9** Clube do Choro. Catch an authentic performance of "Choro", a musical style from Rio, brought to Brasília in the 1960s when the capital was moved from Rio. Clube do Choro is probably the best performance center for Choro in the country.

**10** Chapada dos Veadeiros national park. Located 230 kilometeres (140 miles) from Brasília, this nature reserve is one of the natural wonders of Brazil. It offers great hiking and unique rock formations, incredible canyons and waterfalls and a rich fauna and flora.

## 10 things to do and see in Salvador

1 Pelourinho. Enjoy the architecture and cultural events in Salvador's most-visited square. Give yourself plenty of time to take in all the churches and historic buildings.

2 Igreja and Convento São Francisco. The São Francisco church and convent are probably the most ornate in Brazil and are known for the extensive use of gold leaf on the altar.

3 Igreja de Nosso Senhor do Bonfim (Bonfim church). This important church in Salvador is known for the "washing of the steps" ceremony performed by the masses every year.

4 Try an authentic acarajé in Largo de Santana, Bairro Rio Vermelho. This is a great place to see people and sample an authentic acarajé at one of the sidewalk restaurants. It gets lively at night.

5 Elevador Lacerda and Mercado Modelo. Enjoy the views as you take the Lacerdo elevator down to the old part of Salvador. The Mercado Modelo market, at the base of the elevator, offers excellent meals in addition to the vibrant market.

6 Watch the sunset from Farol da Barra. This popular and lively gathering spot is one of the best places to enjoy the sunset in Salvador.

**7** Attend a mass at the Igreja do Rosário dos Pretos church. The mass is a fascinating mixture of Catholic and African elements.

**8** Tour the beaches north of Salvador. Drive north along the scenic "coconut highway" (Estrada do Coco) and visit the charming beaches such as Itapoã, imortalized by Brazilian poet and songwriter Vinicius de Morães, Flamengo beach and others.

**9** Capoeira. No trip to Bahia would be complete without seeing a performance of this popular Afro-Brazilian martial art and dance called "capoeira".

"Capoeira" in Salvador

**10** Spend the day on Ilha de Itaparica. Just a short boat ride across the mouth of the bay lies the charming island of Itaparica and its sleepy little colonial town and beautiful beaches.

# Food and drink

UNLIKE MOST OTHER countries in the New World, Brazil developed a truly "national" cuisine: a marriage of European, African and indigenous ingredients and flavors. The result is uniquely Brazilian and delicious. Brazilian cuisine is quite regional and the dishes and ingredients change as one travels around the country. As a rule, you can eat very well and inexpensively in most local restaurants at lunchtime, especially if you order the daily special. Dinner is more expensive. You'll find restaurants for all budgets.

Generally speaking, lunch is the biggest meal of the day for Brazilians. Breakfasts in hotels are very substantial with plenty of variety, including fresh fruits and juices, coffee, milk, yoghurt, cakes, rolls, ham, cheese and often scrambled eggs. Brazilians usually have a lighter dinner at around 8 p.m. On weekends people dine out later and it's not uncommon to see restaurants full at midnight with people enjoying their dinner.

São Paulo is the gastronomical capital of Brazil and Latin America. You'll find the options overwhelming and sometimes the prices as well, but the quality and service are top notch.

## Brazilian dishes

It would be a crime not to sample some — or all — of the dishes below while visiting Brazil.

**FEIJOADA** This hearty black bean stew is probably Brazil's best-known dish. It's something of a "national dish" and in places like Rio and São Paulo it is taken very seriously. Feijoada is a black bean stew with pork, sausage and jerked beef, served with rice, farofa (toasted seasoned manioc flour), collard greens sautéed with garlic, oranges cut in slices and hot sauce, all on the side. This can be a cheap or moderately expensive meal. Many neighborhood restaurants serve an inexpensive feijoada on Wednesdays for lunch and it is often served on Saturdays at lunchtime in finer restaurants. It's a great value, very filling and delicious. Order a "caipirinha" with it — a Rio tradition! — or a cold "chopp" (draft beer).

A "feijoada" with all the trimmings

**RODÍZIO DE CARNE/CHURRASCARIA** Another Brazilian first! Foreigners are catching on to this great Brazilian institution and opening "rodízios" in North America and Europe. Rodízios are restaurants — usually quite large — where they serve barbecued meats in an all-you-can-eat system. There is usually a very extensive self-serve salad bar and hot dish area where you can fill your plate as often as you wish. The real treat is the meat, which comes to your table, piping hot off the grill, on large skewers. The waiters flow from table to table, each with a different cut of meat, offering slices of hot meat or sausages, which diners take with their own set of tongs as they are being sliced from the skewers. A word of advice: pace yourself and avoid the temptation to pile your plate up with all the different food at the buffet. You'll notice that Brazilians and "experienced" rodízio diners go easy on the hot buffet, or even dispense with it altogether, to leave more room for the barbecued meat, which is delicious and the reason you're there in the first place.

"Churrasco", the Brazilian barbecue

# FOOD AND DRINK

**COMIDA POR QUILO (KILO)** These restaurants are popular all over Brazil and offer one of the best values going for lunch or dinner. Basically, these are "weigh-your-plate" restaurants. The price per kilo is usually clearly marked at the door so there are no surprises. Generally, kilo restaurants offer a good salad bar and hot dish buffet and some even specialize in barbecued meat, seafood or Brazilian regional cuisine like "comida mineira" (dishes from Minas Gerais). The obvious advantage of these places is that you take and pay for just what you want. Kilo restaurants are usually packed at lunchtime with local working people. Some also open for dinner.

**SALGADINHOS** Brazilian snack food, known as "salgadinhos", can be found almost anywhere. Corner bars, bakeries (padarias), snack bars and even street vendors sell these little pastries which come in various forms. From the Japanese community there is the "pastel", a fried pastry stuffed with meat or other fillings.

"Salgadinhos"

From the Arabic community there is the "esfiha" (meat pastry) and "kibe" (deep fried balls of ground beef and bulgar wheat). Then there are many others like "coxinha" (a soft doughy pastry stuffed with chicken), "empadinha" (small pie pastry filled with meat, chicken or palm heart), "bolinho de queijo" (fried cheese pastry) and the famous "pão de queijo" (baked cheese bread). All are delicious and inexpensive and go great with a cold beer or a Guaraná!

**DOCES** Brazilians really love their sweets, or "doces", as they call them. Most hotels even serve different cakes at breakfast, among other things. Try some of the cakes such as "bolo

"Brigadeiro"

de fubá" (a cake made with cornmeal), "cocada" (a chewy coconut square) and "quindim" (made with egg yolks and coconut). Other typical sweets include "paçoca" (a crumbly sweet peanut square) and the national treasure, "brigadeiro" (chewy chocolate and condensed milk balls rolled in chocolate sprinkles). A common and delicious desert in Brazil is "Romeo e Julieta", a thick slice of guava jelly topped with a slice of white cheese.

Authentic "Acarajé"

**ACARAJÉ** This is Bahia's favorite snack food. Acarajé is a deep-fried pastry made of mashed beans filled with dried shrimp, cashew paste, hot peppers and spices. Outside of Bahia it's hard to find an authentic acarajé, but it's worth looking.

## FOOD AND DRINK

**AÇAÍ** This small, dark purple fruit is the seed from the Açaí palm, native to the Amazon. The external flesh around the seed is ground into a thick, dark purple paste and is used

Harvesting the Açaí fruit

to make juice or served frozen in a bowl (like a slush) called "açaí na tigela" (açaí in a bowl). Açaí has become fashionable in the US and other countries. It's worth trying the real stuff while you're in Brazil.

The "Liberdade" neighbourhood in São Paulo

**JAPANESE FOOD** It's a little-known fact, but Brazil has the largest Japanese community outside Japan. Most of the Japanese settled in the states of São Paulo and Paraná, making the city of São Paulo the largest "Japanese" city outside Japan. Inevitably, the Japanese have contributed to the culinary mosaic of Brazil. Long before sushi became fashionable in North America and Europe, you could find fantastic sushi places scattered around the city of São Paulo and particularly in the Japanese neighborhood of Liberdade. Liberdade is still one of the best places to eat Japanese food in São Paulo.

"Moqueca", a savory seafood stew

**SEAFOOD** Brazil's coast runs from the tropical north to subtropical and cool waters of the south. The result is a great variety of fish and seafood to choose from. The northeast of Brazil has some of the most interesting dishes, such as "moqueca" (fish or other seafood stewed with tomatoes, peppers, coconut milk and spices), "vatapá" (a dish with dried shrimps, coconut milk and cashews) and "bobó de camarão" (a shrimp, manioc and coconut dish). Seafood is typically cooked with coconut milk, peppers, ginger, garlic, onions and tomatoes, among other ingredients and spices. The dishes are varied and delicious. In the south, there is the "tainha na telha" (a whole mullet cooked on a ceramic roof shingle) and "caldeirada de frutos do mar" (seafood stew). All along the coast and in most large cities you can find excellent seafood.

## FOOD AND DRINK

Pizzas cooked in a wood-burning oven

**PIZZA** Don't leave São Paulo without trying the pizza. Other parts of Brazil might have good pizza, but São Paulo, with its huge Italian population, is known for the best pizza. The best places cook their pizzas in wood-burning ovens. The toppings are varied and sometimes "exotic" for North American or European tastes (peas, corn, boiled eggs among others), but there are literally dozens of toppings to choose from. Try a pizza with Catupiry® cheese, a Brazilian national treasure. Brazilians don't normally eat pizza for lunch, only dinner.

**ITALIAN FOOD** You'll find exceptionally good Italian restaurants in the southeast and south of Brazil, especially in São Paulo. The Italian "cantinas" are usually a good choice and offer great food, big servings and a fun and lively atmosphere.

Typical "Cantina" fare

**ARABIC FOOD** Brazil has a large Middle Eastern population that has influenced Brazilian cuisine, especially in the southeast. Esfiha, kibe and tabule are just some of the everyday fare found in restaurants and snack bars. In fact, one of the biggest competitors in the fast food segment is a chain of Arabic fast food restaurants called Habib's.

## Drinking in Brazil

Brazilians are good drinkers, but displays of public drunkenness are rare and frowned upon. Drinking is almost always accompanied with food — either a meal or some finger food. Brazilians drink a fair amount of beer, especially

"Cachaça"

in the summer. Most of the Brazilian beers are light lager-type beers (5% alcohol) with a few options for dark beers. Brewpubs and microbreweries are just now springing up in larger Brazilian cities, but for the most part beer production is dominated by a handful of large brewers.

Brazilians were not big wine drinkers in the past, but this is changing. Wines from Europe, Argentina, Chile and Brazil are widely available, although they're not cheap. Brazilian

## FOOD AND DRINK

wine has improved a great deal in the last decades and it's worthwhile trying a few while in Brazil. The main wine-producing region is in the mountains of Rio Grande do Sul and, more recently, the São Francisco river valley in the northeast. Brazil's national drink is, of course, "cachaça" or "pinga", distilled from sugarcane. There are many small producers who produce fantastic cachaças and it's certainly worth trying some of the good stuff. Nowadays there are sophisticated bars and boutiques that specialize in these finer, small-production quality cachaças. The common supermarket stuff is best used with lime, sugar and ice for making "caipirinhas".

**CAIPIRINHA** The national drink of Brazil is the ubiquitous and delicious "caipirinha". It's made with "cachaça" — also known as "pinga" —, crushed lime slices, sugar and ice. There

"Caipirinha", Brazil's national drink

are variations on the traditional pinga and lime drink that can substitute pinga with vodka, rum or even sake (Japanese rice wine) and other fruits such as passion fruit, kiwi or strawberries in the place of lime.

The Guaraná fruit

**GUARANÁ** Brazil's national soft drink, Guaraná, is made from the mildly stimulating guaraná fruit

43

of the Amazon. In this very sweet and industrialized form, it doesn't really bear much semblance of taste to the real fruit, but it's pretty good all the same.

## Key words

bar: **bar**
beef: **carne**
beer: **cerveja**
bill: **conta**
bottled mineral water: **água mineral**
chicken: **frango**
draft beer: **chopp**
drinks: **bebidas**
fish: **peixe**
food: **comida**
red wine: **vinho tinto**
restaurant: **restaurante**
rice and beans: **arroz e feijão**
salad: **salada**
snack bar, lunch counter: **lanchonete**
tip: **gorjeta**
vegetables: **legumes**
waiter: **garçom**
white wine: **vinho branco**

# Health

### Emergency health care

Brazil has a free public health system in addition to its private network of doctors and hospitals. A traveling foreigner will be well attended by the network of small public clinics and hospitals known as a "Santa Casa da Misericórdia" or simply "Santa Casa". They work on a walk-in basis and no appointment is necessary. Private hospitals will attend foreign visitors via the emergency ward, but payment is necessary and with foreign health insurance it will be bureaucratic. Better to pay in cash and collect later from your insurance company.

General emergency services (like the American 911) can be reached by dialing 192 from anywhere in Brazil.

### Vaccinations

For a complete list of recommended vaccinations see your doctor or the recommendations made by your state health department. In general, vaccinations for the following diseases are recommended for travelers:

**HEPATITIS A AND B** Recommended for all travelers to Brazil.

**MALARIA** Recommended for the states of Acre, Amapá, Amazonas, Maranhão (western part), Mato Grosso (northern part), Pará (except Belém City), Rondônia, Roraima, and Tocantins, and for urban areas within these states, including the cities of Porto Velho, Boa Vista, Macapá, Manaus, Santarém and Marabá.

**YELLOW FEVER** Recommended for all areas of Acre, Amapá, Amazonas, Distrito Federal (including the capital city of Brasília), Goiás, Maranhão, Mato Grosso, Mato Grosso do Sul, Minas Gerais, Pará, Rondônia, Roraima, Tocantins, and designated areas of the following states: northwest and west Bahia, central and west Paraná, southwest Piauí, northwest and west central Rio Grande do Sul (including Porto Alegre), far west Santa Catarina, and north and south central São Paulo.

**TYPHOID** Recommended if planning on straying off the beaten path and eating outside hotels and restaurants.

**RABIES** Especially if your planned activities include contact with wild animals and bats.

**MEASLES, MUMPS, RUBELLA (MMR)** Recommended especially to anyone born after 1956.

**TETANUS-DIPHTHERIA** (Requires a booster every 10 years.)

## Special health risks

**DENGUE FEVER** Dengue fever is transmitted by the mosquito *Aedes aegypti* and can be fatal in some cases. There is no vaccination for Dengue. Dengue is common in many parts of Brazil, especially in the summer months, when outbreaks can sweep through areas quickly. If you know you are in a Dengue region, take extra care by using plenty of insect repellant and sleeping with either a mosquito net or a plug-in mosquito repellant (called a "protetor" in Brazil). Dengue symptoms can include fever, muscle aches and pain behind the eyes. The symptoms are often mistaken for flu symptoms. Aspirins and other medicines that contain acetylsalicylic acid should never be taken if Dengue is suspected as it can aggravate hemorrhaging. Tylenol® is fine though. Any fever is cause to visit a doctor if you are in region that is known to have Dengue.

**DIARRHEA** Diarrhea can be caused by the change in water or diet or by the presence of contaminants in the food or water. In any case, the risk of dehydration is great, especially among small children. Persistent diarrhea or the presence of blood in stools is cause to visit a doctor.

## Key words

dentist: **dentista**

doctor: **médico**

free public hospital or clinic: **Santa Casa/ hospital público**

medicine: **remédio**

pharmacy: **farmácia**

BRAZIL IN A NUTSHELL

# Holidays and special dates in Brazil

**New year's eve celebration in Copacabana**

## Brazil observes the following national holidays

**NEW YEAR** - January 1

**CARNIVAL** - February/ March (Carnival occurs seven weeks before Easter so the exact dates vary from year to year. Monday and Tuesday are the "official" holidays, but celebrations begin on Friday evening and end at midday on Ash Wednesday, when shops and services normally re-open.)

**GOOD FRIDAY** - March/ April (movable) two days before Easter Sunday

**TIRADENTES** - April 21

**LABOUR DAY** - May 1

**CORPUS CHRISTI** - May/ June (movable) sixty days after Easter Sunday

**INDEPENDENCE DAY** - September 7

**OUR LADY OF APARECIDA** (Patroness of Brazil) - October 12

**ALL SOULS' DAY ("DIA DE FINADOS")** - November 2

**REPUBLIC DAY** - November 15

**CHRISTMAS** - December 25

HOLIDAYS AND SPECIAL DATES IN BRAZIL

There are some state and municipal holidays as well. Most cities have a "city birthday" which is a municipal holiday.

Besides the national holidays, there are regional festivals, religious festivals and traditional parties held all over the country. Visitors can get information from local tourist offices to check the cultural agenda during their stay. Some of the larger festivals and celebrations in Brazil are described below.

## Carnival

February/ March (movable). Considered the biggest party on Earth! Brazil stops for four days to party and put on a show. Carnival is celebrated everywhere in Brazil, but the most famous carnival celebrations are in Rio de Janeiro (RJ), Salvador (BA), Olinda (PE), Recife (PE) and São Paulo (SP). Practically every town has parades, shows and parties that go on all night. There are usually daytime "matinês" with parades and music just for children. It's very hard to find a hotel room or transportation during carnival without a reservation, so booking your itinerary well in advance is essential.

Carnival in Rio

### "Carnaval fora de época"

Movable. Some cities offer an "out-of-season" carnival for those who can't wait a whole year for regular carnival. Recife (PE) has its famous Recifolia and many other cities offer a "second" carnival at different times of the year, with shows, parades and events.

### Boi-bumbá / Bumba meu boi

June and July. This popular festival in the state of Maranhão dates back to the 18th century. There are colorful parades with cow effigies, dancing and afro-Brazilian music. Elsewhere in the north and northeast there are variations of the Bumba meu boi celebration.

Boi-Bumbá

### Festival de Parintins

June. The Festival de Parintins is the Amazonian variation of the Bumba meu boi festival and is the second largest popular festival in the country. It mixes elements of the Boi-bumbá and elements of indigenous Amazonian folklore. For

HOLIDAYS AND SPECIAL DATES IN BRAZIL

three days revelers, dancers and storytellers parade two giant cow effigies on decorated floats, one red called "Garantido" and the other blue called "Caprichoso" for the crowds and judges to see. A panel of judges declares the winner on the last evening of the celebration.

"Garantido" and "Caprichoso"

## Festa do Divino

Movable. This popular religious celebration, held 50 days after Easter on Pentecost Sunday, was brought

Festa do Divino

51

to Brazil by the Portuguese Jesuits. It is celebrated all over Brazil, but some cities are known for their celebrations, like Mogi das Cruzes (SP), Paraty (RJ) and Pirenópolis (GO). Depending on the place, the festival has masses, fireworks, processions, music, feasts and re-enactments of battles between Christians and Moors.

### Círio de Nazaré

The second Sunday of October. The largest Catholic procession in the world. It dates back to 1793. More than 2 million people participate in the event every year in Belém do Pará (PA).

Círio de Nazaré

### Congado

October. The Congado (also known as Congo or Congada) is an Afro-Brazilian religious celebration that celebrates the life of Saint Benedict, Our Lady of the Rosary and the battle between Carlos Magno and the invading Moors.

HOLIDAYS AND SPECIAL DATES IN BRAZIL

It is celebrated in many parts of Brazil. The festival has processions of saints, dancing, music, parades and it culminates in the "crowning" of the king of the Congo.

### Festa junina

June. This traditional "winter" party is celebrated all over Brazil. It coincides with June 24 (the day of Saint John the Baptist), but not necessarily on that day. Throughout the month of June there are parties. The celebrations include square dancing, dancing around the Maypole, feasts, releasing small hot-air balloons and bonfires at night.

Congado

Festa junina

## Oktoberfest

October. The town of Blumenau (SC), which was settled by Germans, hosts the biggest Oktoberfest in the Americas, modeled on the famous one in Munich. For 18 days, German food and beer flow freely to the more than half a million revelers. The town also hosts parades, dances, shows and presentations of local folklore.

The biggest "Oktoberfest" in the Americas

## Key words

holiday: **feriado**
music: **música**
parade: **desfile, parada**
party, celebration: **festa, celebração**
performance: **show**
show: **show**
stage: **palco**

BRAZIL IN A NUTSHELL

# Money matters

**Brazilian coins and banknotes**

THE CURRENCY OF Brazil is the Real and it is abbreviated as BRL or R$. The plural of Real in Portuguese is "Reais". They are pronounced as "hey-al" and "hey-ice" in Brazilian Portuguese. Brazil has a floating exchange rate, so the exchange rate can move up or down, depending on the day.

IN 2010 BRAZIL launched new banknotes, which are in circulation with the old ones. The main change is the size of the bills, but some figures and the colors remain the same. Both banknotes, old and new, are accepted.

**Foreign exchange**

Foreign currencies and traveler's checks can be exchanged at a "casa de câmbio" (foreign exchange bureau) and some banks. Airport exchange houses accept most foreign currencies, but the exchange rate is not usually the most favorable. If you are traveling with cash in a currency other than the US dollar, Euro or the Argentine peso, be warned that you will encounter far fewer places to exchange your money. Many places will accept US dollars but not other foreign currencies. All the major Brazilian banks have some designated branches that buy and sell foreign currency, but they are few and far between when you leave the big cities and tourist areas. In smaller towns it may be difficult to find a place to exchange your money, especially if it's not the US dollar. Some stores and restaurants in tourist areas will take US dollars or Argentine pesos as payment, but always ask in advance.

New Brazilian banknotes

## Credit and bank (debit) cards

The easiest way to deal with getting money is using your bank (debit) or credit card. All the major credit cards are accepted in Brazil (Visa, MasterCard, American Express, Diners). You should have no problem using your credit card in stores or restaurants, even in small towns. Brazilian banks operate under their own national interbank system and often under international networks as well (like Plus and Cirrus), but not all branches of any given bank will have ATMs that take foreign bank cards. Look for your bank card logo on ATMs. Outside of bigger cities and tourist areas it might be harder to find ATMs that will work with foreign bank cards.

## Traveler's checks

Traveler's checks are not widely accepted and will probably bring you more headaches than benefits in Brazil. Your credit card and bank card are your best bets for getting a constant stream of cash while traveling in Brazil.

## Tipping

Normally the service is included in your restaurant bill. A 10% "service charge", the "tip", is added on to the total. Always check that it is added to your bar or restaurant bill as some places don't include it automatically. In such cases you should add 10% for the waiter. It isn't necessary or even common to leave anything more than the obligatory 10%, but a little extra for excellent service is appreciated. In hotels, it is common to tip the porters and service staff if you have received good service.

## Key words

ATM: **caixa eletrônico**
bank: **banco**
bank branch: **agência**
bank card: **cartão de débito**
cent: **centavo**
charge, fee: **taxa**
credit card: **cartão de crédito**
currency: **moeda**
exchange rate: **taxa de câmbio**
foreign exchange bureau: **casa de câmbio**
money: **dinheiro**
tip: **gorjeta**

# Crime and security in Brazil

**Travel tips**

Brazil has its share of crime and unfortunately tourists are not immune. The common sense tips below should be enough to keep you out of trouble.

- Leave your passport (carry a xerox) and valuables like expensive watches and jewelry at the hotel when you go out. The less you have on display, the better.

- Don't bring valuables to the beach. Pocket money can be kept in a waterproof tube for swimming or even in a bathing suit pocket. You won't have a wet bill refused when buying an ice cream or a beer on the beach.

- At night, especially in cities, stick to well-lit places and streets with other pedestrians. Unlit urban beaches are often unsafe at night. When in doubt, ask a local.

- Consider carrying a small amount of cash rather than credit or bank cards to avoid "express kidnappings" where victims are forced to withdraw money at ATMs to pay their "ransom". Carrying enough for the day or a meal out plus a little extra could be safer.

CRIME AND SECURITY IN BRAZIL

▸ Airports in Brazil are safe. Bus terminals, not always. Watch your bag at bus stations.

▸ The "OK" hand gesture, using the index finger and thumb in a circle, does not mean "perfect" or "OK" in Brazil. It's a rude gesture used to insult someone. Instead, use the "thumbs up" gesture.

## Key words

crime: **crime**
police officer: **policial**
police: **polícia**
safe (hotel safe or strongbox for valuables): **cofre**
safe: **seguro**
thief: **ladrão**
valuables: **objetos de valor**

# PART 2

# Communicating in Brazil

BRAZIL IN A NUTSHELL

# Survival language

**Basic interaction**

Hi. » **Oi.**

Hello. » **Olá, alô.** (telephone)

Goodbye. » **Tchau.**

Good morning. » **Bom dia.**

Good afternoon. » **Boa tarde.**

Good evening. » **Boa noite.**

Good night. » **Boa noite.**

Yes. » **Sim.**

No. » **Não.**

OK. » **Está bem, certo.**

Please. » **Por favor.**

Thank you. » **Obrigado.** (if you're a man);

**Obrigada.** (if you're a woman)

You're welcome. » **De nada.**

Excuse me. » **Com licença.**

Sorry. » **Desculpa.**

## Greetings

Hi. » **Oi.**

Hello. (telephone) » **Alô.**

How are you? » **Tudo bem?, Como vai?**

Nice to meet you. » **Prazer em conhecer.**

Pleasure to meet you. » **Prazer em conhecer.**

## Good-byes

Goodbye. (formal) » **Adeus.**

Bye. (informal) » **Tchau, Até logo.**

See you later. » **Até mais, Até logo.**

See you tomorrow. » **Até amanhã.**

Till next time. » **Até a próxima.**

Have a nice weekend. » **Bom fim de semana.**

Thanks for a good time. » **Obrigado pela companhia.**

All the best. » **Tudo de bom.**

Thanks for inviting me. » **Obrigado pelo convite.**

## Comprehension phrases and questions

I don't understand. » **Não estou entendendo.**

I don't know. » **Eu não sei.**

I don't speak Portuguese. » **Eu não falo português.**

Do you speak English? » **Você fala inglês?**

What did you say? » **O que você disse?**

Please speak slowly. » **Por favor, fale devagar.**

Just a little bit. » **Só um pouquinho.**

Sorry, I don't understand. » **Me desculpe, eu não entendi.**

Can you write that down for me please? » **Você pode escrever isso pra mim, por favor?**

Can you repeat that, please? » **Pode repetir, por favor?**

I think so. » **Acho que sim.**

I don't believe so. » **Acredito que não.**

A moment, please. » **Um momento, por favor.**

No problem. » **Não tem problema.**

Absolutely. » **Com certeza.**

I'm learning Portuguese. » **Eu estou aprendendo português.**

What's the Portuguese for this? » **Como se diz isso em português?**

What do you call this in Portuguese? » **Como se chama isto em português?**

What does it mean? » **O que significa isso?**

## Small talk and plesantries

How are you? » **Tudo bem?**

Fine. » **Bem.**

Where are you from? » **De onde você é?**

I'm from Germany. » **Eu sou da Alemanha.**

I'm Canadian. » **Eu sou canadense.**

My name's John. » **Meu nome é John.**

What's your name? » **Qual é o seu nome?**

Nice to meet you. » **Prazer em conhecê-lo(a).**

Where do you live? » **Onde você mora?**

Where are you from? » **De onde você é?**

Where do you work? » **Onde você trabalha?**

What do you do? » **Você trabalha em quê?**

How old are you? » **Quantos anos você tem?**

Are you Brazilian? » **Você é brasileiro?** (to a man); **Você é brasileira?** (to a woman)

Do you have children? » **Você tem filhos?**

# Transportation

## Airport

Where is the Air Canada counter? » **Onde fica o balcão da empresa Air Canada?**

I want a roundtrip/ return ticket to Rio, please. » **Quero uma passagem de ida e volta para o Rio, por favor.**

I want a one-way ticket to Porto Seguro, please. » **Eu quero uma passagem só de ida para Porto Seguro, por favor.**

How much is it? » **Quanto é?**

I'd like a window seat. » **Eu gostaria de um assento do lado da janela.**

I'd like an aisle seat. » **Eu gostaria de um assento do lado do corredor.**

Where can I exchange some money? » **Onde eu posso trocar dinheiro?**

BRAZIL IN A NUTSHELL

Where is the check-in counter? » **Onde fica o balcão de check-in?**

What is the departure time? » **Qual é o horário de partida?**

What is the gate number? » **Qual o número do portão de embarque?**

## Key words

airport: **aeroporto**
airline counter: **balcão da empresa aérea**
airplane: **avião**
bag: **mala**
baggage claim area: **terminal de bagagem**
blanket: **cobertor**
boarding area: **área de embarque**
boarding pass: **cartão de embarque**
carousel: **esteira**
carry-on bag: **bagagem de mão**
check-in counter: **balcão de embarque, balcão de check-in**
customs: **alfândega**
customs declaration form: **formulário de declaração para a alfândega**
customs officer: **agente de alfândega**
exit: **saída**
flight: **voo**
flight attendant: **aeromoça, comissário de voo**
gate: **portão de embarque**
information desk: **balcão de informações**
in transit: **em trânsito**
luggage: **bagagem**
luggage cart: **carrinho de bagagem**
overhead compartment: **compartimento de bagagem de mão**
passenger: **passageiro**
passport: **passaporte**
pilot: **piloto, comandante**
plane: **avião**
seat belt: **cinto de segurança**
seat: **assento, poltrona**
ticket: **bilhete, passagem**
trip: **viagem**

DANIEL LOISELLE / ISTOCKPHOTO

## Bus station and buses

Where's the ticket office? » **Onde fica a bilheteria?**

Is there a bus stop near here? » **Tem algum ponto de ônibus por aqui?**

Does the number 55 bus stop here? » **O ônibus 55 para aqui?**

Where does this bus go? » **Para onde este ônibus vai?**

Is this the bus to Salvador? » **Este é o ônibus que vai para Salvador?**

How much is the ticket to São Paulo? » **Quanto custa o bilhete para São Paulo?**

What time does the bus leave? » **A que horas o ônibus parte?**

Is this seat taken? » **Este lugar está ocupado?**

Can I sit here? » **Posso sentar aqui?**

You're in my seat. » **Você está no meu lugar.**

Which platform? » **Qual plataforma?**

When does the next bus come by? » **Quando vem o próximo ônibus?**

What time does the next bus to Rio leave? » **A que horas sai o próximo ônibus para o Rio?**

What's the schedule to São Paulo? » **Qual é o horário do ônibus para São Paulo?**

I'd like a ticket to Recife, please. » **Eu quero uma passagem para Recife, por favor.**

How long is the trip? » **Quanto tempo de viagem?**

Is there a window seat? » **Tem lugar do lado da janela?**

I want to get off here. » **Eu quero descer aqui.**

## Key words

bus: **ônibus**
bus driver: **motorista de ônibus**
bus station, bus terminal: **rodoviária**
bus stop: **ponto de ônibus**
platform: **plataforma**
route: **rota**
schedule: **horário**
ticket: **bilhete, passagem**
window: **janela**

Magnificent views on the train from Curitiba to Paranaguá (PR)

### Train and subway

Is there a subway station near here? » **Tem estação de metrô aqui perto?**

Where is the train station? » **Onde fica a estação de trem?**

Does the subway go to Rodoviária do Tietê? » **O metrô vai para a Rodoviária do Tietê?**

TRANSPORTATION

Where is the ticket counter? » **Onde fica a bilheteria?**
Where does the train leave from? » **De onde o trem parte?**
What time does the train leave? » **A que horas o trem parte?**

## Key words

platform: **plataforma**
schedule: **horário**
subway, underground: **metrô**
ticket: **bilhete, passagem**
train station: **estação de trem**
train: **trem**

## Car rental

Is there a car rental agency near here? » **Tem alguma locadora de carros por aqui?**
I'd like to rent a car. » **Eu gostaria de alugar um carro.**
How much is the car per day? » **Quanto é a diária do carro?**
I want a car for ten days. » **Eu quero um carro para dez dias.**
Do you have an economy car? » **Você tem um carro básico?**
Do you have a full-size car? » **Você tem um carro grande?**

The scenic Rio-Santos highway offers stunning views of the coast

Does the car have air conditioning? » **O carro tem ar-condicionado?**

Is the mileage unlimited? » **A quilometragem é ilimitada?**

How much do the extra kilometers cost? » **Quanto custa a quilometragem extra?**

Is the insurance included in the price? » **O seguro está incluso no valor?**

How much is the insurance? » **Quanto é o seguro?**

Where can I drop off the car? » **Onde eu posso deixar o carro?**

## Key words

car park, parking lot: **estacionamento**
compact: **compacto**
convertible: **conversível**
driver's license: **carteira de motorista, habilitação**
ethanol: **álcool**
gas station, petrol station: **posto de gasolina**
gasoline: **gasolina**
minivan: **minivan**
oil: **óleo**
sedan: **sedã**
speed: **velocidade**
sports car: **carro esportivo**
station wagon: **perua**
sunroof: **teto solar**
SUV: **utilitário esportivo, SUV**

## Taxi

Can you call me a taxi? » **Você pode chamar um táxi?**

Are you free? » **Você está livre?**

How much is the fare to the Maracanã Stadium? » **Quanto é a corrida até o Estádio do Maracanã?**

TRANSPORTATION

I want to go to the Copacabana Palace Hotel. » **Quero ir ao Hotel Copacabana Palace.**

How much is the fare? » **Quanto é a corrida?**

How much would it be to the Cristo Redentor? » **Quanto ficaria até o Cristo Redentor?**

Avenida Paulista, please. » **Avenida Paulista, por favor.**

Take me to this address please. » **Me leve até este endereço, por favor.**

Take me to the Morumbi Stadium please. » **Para o Estádio do Morumbi, por favor.**

How far is it to the Estádio do Maracanã? » **Qual distância até o Estádio do Maracanã?**

Can you hurry up a little? » **Dá para apressar um pouquinho?**

Can you slow down a bit? » **Dá para ir um pouco mais devagar?**

Here is fine. » **Aqui está ótimo.**

Just drop me off at the corner please. » **Na esquina está bom, por favor.**

How much is it? » **Quanto é?**

Can I have a receipt? » **Você me dá um recibo?**

Keep the change. Thanks. » **Fique com o troco. Obrigado.**

## Key words

taxi driver: **motorista de táxi**
taxi: **táxi**
change: **troco**
corner: **esquina**
meter: **taxímetro**
taxi stand: **ponto de táxi**
traffic: **trânsito**
traffic jam: **congestionamento**
traffic light: **semáforo**
trunk: **porta-malas**

# Money matters and shopping

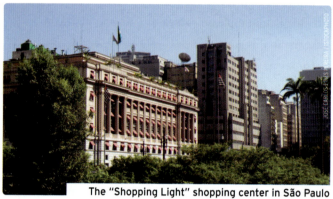

The "Shopping Light" shopping center in São Paulo

**Foreign exchange and banking**

Where can I exchange some money? » **Onde eu posso trocar dinheiro?**

Is there a bank near here? » **Tem um banco por aqui?**

Is there an ATM near here? » **Tem um caixa eletrônico aqui perto?**

What's the US dollar exchange rate today? » **Qual é a cotação do dólar hoje?**

Do you accept US dollars? » **Você aceita dólares?**

**Shopping**

Is there a shopping center near here? » **Tem algum shopping center aqui perto?**

Where can I buy some clothes? » **Onde eu posso comprar algumas roupas?**

Is there a supermarket near here? » **Tem algum supermercado aqui perto?**

## MONEY MATTERS AND SHOPPING

I am just looking, thanks. » **Estou só olhando, obrigado.**

How much is it? » **Quanto custa?**

Can I see that one? » **Posso ver aquele ali?**

It's too expensive! » **É muito caro!**

Have you got a cheaper one? » **Você tem um mais barato?**

Can you give me a discount if I pay in cash? » **Tem desconto para pagamento à vista?**

Do you take credit cards? » **Vocês trabalham com cartão de crédito?**

Can I try it on? » **Posso experimentar?**

Do you have it in a larger size? » **Você tem em tamanho maior?**

Do you have it in a smaller size? » **Você tem em tamanho menor?**

Do you have it in another color? » **Você tem em outra cor?**

I'll take it. » **Vou levar.**

Can I have a receipt? » **Você me dá um recibo?**

---

## Key words

account number: **número da conta**
ATM: **caixa eletrônico**
balance (on account): **saldo**
bank machine: **caixa eletrônico**
bank teller: **caixa**
bank transfer: **transferência**
bank card: **cartão de débito**
change: **troco**
check, cheque: **cheque**
checkbook, chequebook: **talão de cheques**
checking account: **conta corrente**
closed: **fechado**
coins: **moedas**
credit card: **cartão de crédito**
debit card: **cartão de débito**

BRAZIL IN A NUTSHELL

deposit: **depósito**
discount: **desconto**
manager: **gerente**
open: **aberto**
PIN number: **senha**
receipt: **recibo**
savings account: **poupança**
security guard: **segurança**
shop assistant: **vendedor**
shopping bag: **sacola**
statement (bank): **extrato**
withdrawal: **saque**

## Key words: the mall

bookstore: **livraria**
candy store: **doceria**
department store: **loja de departamentos**
directory, mall map: **painel de informações**
electronics store: **loja de artigos eletrônicos**
elevator: **elevador**
escalator: **escada rolante**
exit: **saída**
food court: **praça de alimentação**
hair salon: **salão de beleza**
ice cream stand: **quiosque de sorvete**
information booth: **balcão de informações**
jewelry store: **joalheria**
music store: **loja de CDs**
pet store: **loja de animais**
shoe store: **loja de calçados**
stairs: **escadas**
toy store: **loja de brinquedos**
travel agency: **agência de viagens**
video store: **loja de vídeos**

# At the hotel

The stately Copacabana Palace Hotel in Rio

## Questions and phrases

Can you recommend a hotel? » **Você pode me indicar um hotel?**
I'd like a single room. » **Eu gostaria de um quarto de solteiro.**
I'd like a double room. » **Eu gostaria de um quarto de casal.**
I'd like a room with two single beds. » **Eu gostaria de um quarto com duas camas de solteiro.**
For two nights. » **Por duas noites.**
I'd like a room with a bath. » **Eu gostaria de um quarto com banheiro.**
How much is the room? » **Quanto fica o quarto?**
Is there room service? » **Tem serviço de quarto?**
Is breakfast included? » **O café da manhã está incluído?**

Does the room have cable TV? » **O quarto tem TV a cabo?**

It's fine. How much is it? » **Está bom. Quanto é?**

It's too expensive. » **É caro demais.**

Do you have anything cheaper? » **Você tem algo mais barato?**

Do you have anything nicer? » **Você tem algo mais confortável?**

I want to check in. » **Eu quero fazer o check-in.**

I have a reservation in the name of Adam Smith. » **Eu tenho uma reserva em nome de Adam Smith.**

I'll be staying until 28th July. » **Eu vou ficar até o dia 28 de julho.**

Can I have my key? » **A chave, por favor.**

Are there any messages for me? » **Tem algum recado pra mim?**

What time is check out? » **Qual é o horário de check-out?**

Can I have my bill, please? » **A conta, por favor.**

Does the room have a phone? » **O quarto tem telefone?**

Does the room have air conditioning? » **O quarto tem ar-condicionado?**

Does the hotel have a pool? » **O hotel tem piscina?**

Can I leave some things in the hotel safe? » **Posso guardar algumas coisas no cofre do hotel?**

What time is breakfast? » **A que horas é o café da manhã?**

Is there a restaurant? » **Tem um restaurante?**

Can I have a bath towel? » **Quero uma toalha de banho, por favor.**

Can I have some soap? » **Quero sabonetes, por favor.**

Can I make a telephone call? » **Posso dar um telefonema?**

Can you wake me up at 7 o'clock? » **Você pode me acordar às 7 horas?**

Can you clean my room? » **Você pode limpar o meu quarto?**

Can you call me a taxi? » **Você pode chamar um táxi pra mim?**

AT THE HOTEL

## Problems

The TV isn't working. » A TV não está funcionando.

There's no hot water. » Não tem água quente.

The air conditioning isn't working. » O ar-condicionado não está funcionando.

I'd like to change rooms, please. » Eu gostaria de trocar de quarto, por favor.

## Key words

air conditioning: **ar-condicionado**

bellhop: **carregador de bagagem**

bill: **conta**

breakfast: **café da manhã**

chambermaid: **camareira**

desk clerk: **recepcionista**

dinner: **jantar**

doorman: **porteiro**

front desk: **recepção**

guest: **hóspede**

hall: **corredor**

intercom: **interfone**

ice: **gelo**

key: **chave**

lobby: **saguão**

lunch: **almoço**

meeting room: **sala de conferência**

minibar: **frigobar**

pool: **piscina**

room service: **serviço de quarto**

snacks: **salgadinhos**

suitcase, bag: **mala**

valet parking: **serviço de manobrista**

BRAZIL IN A NUTSHELL

# On the telephone

"Orelhão" (Public telephone)

**Questions and phrases**

Is there a payphone (public phone) near here? » **Tem um telefone público por aqui?**

I need to make a long distance call (within Brazil). » **Eu preciso fazer uma ligação interurbana.**

I need to make an international call. » **Eu preciso fazer uma ligação internacional.**

May I use your telephone? » **Posso usar seu telefone?**

Can I make a collect call? » **Posso fazer uma ligação a cobrar?**

I need to make a local call. » **Eu preciso fazer uma ligação local.**

What is the area code for São Paulo? » **Qual é o código de área de São Paulo?**

## ON THE TELEPHONE

Can you place a call for me? » **Você pode fazer uma ligação para mim?**

Please ask for Mr Smith. » **Por favor, peça para falar com o Sr. Smith.**

I'd like to make a long distance call to Washington, USA. » **Eu gostaria de fazer uma ligação internacional para Washington, Estados Unidos.**

Is there a mobile signal here? » **Tem sinal de celular aqui?**

## Speaking on the phone

Hello. » **Alô.**

Good bye. » **Tchau.**

Is Ms Brown there? » **A Sra. Brown está?**

This is Joe speaking. » **Aqui quem fala é o Joe.**

Can you tell Peter to call me back? » **Você pode pedir para o Peter me ligar?**

Can you tell John to call me on my mobile? » **Você pode pedir para o John me ligar no meu celular?**

Can you tell Janet to call me at my hotel? » **Você pode pedir para a Janet me ligar no hotel?**

My telephone number is 3567 9887. » **O meu telefone é 3567 9887.**

My mobile phone number is 8889 9009. » **O número do meu celular é 8889 9009.**

The number at my hotel is 4693-2123. » **O telefone do meu hotel é 4693-2123.**

Do you speak English? » **Você fala inglês?**

Is there anyone there who speaks English? » **Tem alguém aí que fala inglês?**

I don't understand. » **Eu não estou entendendo.**

I don't speak Portuguese. » **Eu não falo português.**

Can you repeat that? » **Você pode repetir?**

## BRAZIL IN A NUTSHELL

Can you speak slower? » **Você pode falar mais devagar?**

Can I leave a message for Damion? » **Posso deixar uma mensagem para o Damion?**

Tell Lucy that I called. » **Diga para a Lucy que eu liguei.**

Hello, this is Tom. May I speak to Allan? » **Alô. Aqui é o Tom. Posso falar com o Allan?**

Hello. Extension 286, please. » **Alô. Ramal 286, por favor.**

Can you transfer me, please? » **Você pode me transferir, por favor?**

Can you take a message? » **Você pode anotar um recado?**

I'll call again later. » **Eu ligo mais tarde.**

Hello. I'd like to talk to the manager. » **Alô. Eu queria falar com o gerente.**

Hello. May I talk to Sean? » **Alô. Posso falar com o Sean?**

It's 055 33 5676 5890. » **Aqui é do 055 33 5676 5890.**

Sorry. Wrong number. » **Desculpe. Foi engano.**

What time will he come back? » **A que horas ele volta?**

Speak louder, please! » **Fala mais alto, por favor!**

I've been calling, but I can't get through. » **Só chama, mas ninguém atende.**

The call fell through. » **Caiu a ligação.**

## Key words

answering machine: **secretária eletrônica**

area code (outside Brazil): **DDI (= discagem direta internacional)**

area code (within Brazil): **DDD (= discagem direta a distância)**

busy (telephone): **ocupado**

cellular phone: **telefone celular**

## ON THE TELEPHONE

collect call: **ligação a cobrar**

dial tone: **sinal**

extension: **ramal**

international call: **ligação internacional**

local call: **ligação local**

long distance call: **ligação interurbana**

mobile phone: **celular**

mobile signal: **sinal de celular**

operator: **telefonista**

pay phone: **orelhão, telefone público**

phone card: **cartão telefônico**

telephone: **telefone**

# Health issues and pharmacy

**Questions and phrases**

Where is the pharmacy? » **Onde fica a farmácia?**

Is there a hospital near here? » **Tem algum hospital por aqui?**

Can you take me to the hospital? » **Você pode me levar ao hospital?**

I need to see a doctor. » **Eu preciso de um médico.**

Can I see a doctor? » **Posso falar com o médico?**

Can I see the dentist? » **Posso falar com o dentista?**

I'd like to make an appointment to see the doctor. » **Eu gostaria de marcar uma consulta com o médico.**

It's an emergency. » **É uma emergência.**

I need a prescription. » **Eu preciso de uma receita médica.**

Can you recommend something for sunburn? » **Você pode me recomendar algo para queimadura de sol?**

Do you have something for insect bites? » **Você tem alguma coisa para picadas de inseto?**

Can you have a look at my throat? » **Você pode examinar a minha garganta?**

**Ailments and symptoms**

I have a fever. » **Estou com febre.**

I have a stomach ache. » **Estou com dor de estômago.**

I have a headache. » **Estou com dor de cabeça.**

I have a sore throat. » **Estou com dor de garganta.**

I have an ear ache. » **Estou com dor de ouvido.**

HEALTH ISSUES AND PHARMACY

I have a tooth ache. » **Estou com dor de dente.**

I'm diabetic. » **Eu sou diabético.**

I have asthma. » **Eu tenho asma.**

I have high blood pressure. » **Eu tenho pressão alta.**

I have low blood pressure. » **Eu tenho pressão baixa.**

Do you have something for intestinal parasites? » **Você tem algo para combater parasitas intestinais?**

I'm congested. » **Estou congestionado.**

I'm having difficulty breathing. » **Estou com dificuldades para respirar.**

I'm allergic to penicillin. » **Eu sou alérgico a penicilina.**

I feel weak. » **Estou me sentindo fraco.**

I have pain here. » **Estou sentindo uma dor aqui.**

I have diarrhea. » **Estou com diarreia.**

I feel nauseous. » **Estou com enjoo.**

I'm constipated. » **Estou com o intestino preso.**

I have chest pain. » **Estou com uma dor no peito.**

I feel dizzy. » **Estou sentindo tontura.**

I don't feel well. » **Eu não estou me sentindo bem.**

It seems to be infected. » **Parece que está infeccionado.**

I have a rash. » **Eu estou com uma irritação na pele.**

It's swollen. » **Está inchado.**

I think it's broken. » **Eu acho que está quebrado.**

## Key words: parts of the body

arm: **braço**

back: **costas**

blood: **sangue**

bowel: **intestino**

chest: **peito**

eyes: **olhos**

## BRAZIL IN A NUTSHELL

▶ **Parts of the body**

foot: **pé**
glands: **glândulas**
hand: **mão**
head: **cabeça**
heart: **coração**
leg: **perna**
muscle: **músculo**
stomach: **estômago**
stools: **fezes**
throat: **garganta**
urine: **urina**

# **Key words:** medicines and pharmacy products

anti-allergic: **antialérgico**
antibiotic: **antibiótico**
anti-inflammatory: **anti-inflamatório**
aspirin: **aspirina**
cold medicine: **remédio para resfriado**
conditioner: **condicionador**
condoms: **camisinhas**
decongestant: **descongestionante**
deodorant: **desodorante**
diarrhea medicine: **remédio para diarreia**
eye drops: **colírio**
insect repellent: **repelente**
laxative: **laxante**
moisturizer: **creme hidratante**
razor: **gilete, lâmina de barbear**
shampoo: **xampu**
soap: **sabonete**
sun screen: **protetor solar**
tampons: **absorventes**
toothbrush: **escova de dente**
toothpaste: **pasta de dente**
Tylenol®: **Tylenol®**

## Key words

cold: **resfriado**
dentist: **dentista**
dentist's appointment: **consulta com o dentista**
disease: **doença**
doctor: **médico**
doctor's appointment: **consulta médica**
emergency: **emergência**
flu: **gripe**
hospital: **hospital**
illness: **doença**
medicine: **remédio**
nurse: **enfermeira**
pharmacy: **farmácia**
sick: **doente**

# Food and eating out

**Questions and phrases**

Can you recommend a good restaurant? » Você pode me indicar um bom restaurante?

Is there a restaurant near here? » Tem algum restaurante por aqui?

Is there a snack bar near here? » Tem alguma lanchonete por aqui?

I'd like a table for two. » Eu gostaria de uma mesa para dois.

Do you have a table on the terrace? » Você tem uma mesa no terraço?

I would like a table in the non-smoking section. » Eu gostaria de uma mesa na área de não fumantes.

I would like a table in the smoking section. » Eu gostaria de uma mesa na área de fumantes.

I would like a table by the window. » Eu gostaria de uma mesa ao lado da janela.

Can I see the menu? » Posso ver o cardápio?

Can I see the wine list? » Posso ver a carta de vinhos?

Sidewalk cafés

# FOOD AND EATING OUT

Can I see the dessert menu? » **Posso ver o menu de sobremesas?**

What kind of fruit juice do you have? » **Que tipo de suco de fruta vocês têm?**

What do you recommend? » **O que você recomenda?**

What's today's special? » **Qual é o prato do dia?**

How much is it? » **Quanto custa?**

Is it grilled? » **É grelhado?**

Is it fried? » **É frito?**

Does it come with a salad? » **Vem com salada?**

Can we share a plate? » **Dá pra duas pessoas?**

Do you have any vegetarian dishes? » **Vocês têm pratos vegetarianos?**

I am a vegetarian. » **Eu sou vegetariano.**

Can you prepare my meal without any salt? » **Você pode preparar o meu prato sem sal?**

Are there any low-fat dishes? » **Tem algum prato de baixo teor de gordura?**

Do you have wheelchair access? » **Vocês têm acesso para cadeirantes?**

Does the dish have hot peppers? » **O prato tem pimenta?**

Can I see the menu again? » **Posso ver o cardápio novamente?**

How long will it take? » **Fica pronto em quanto tempo?**

I'm in a bit of a hurry. » **Estou com um pouco de pressa.**

Where is the bathroom? » **Onde fica o banheiro?**

Can you call the waiter? » **Você pode chamar o garçom?**

That looks delicious. » **Parece gostoso.**

I'll have the chicken. » **Eu vou querer frango.**

Can I have a bottle of mineral water? » **Você me traz uma garrafa de água mineral?**

Can I have another? » **Mais um por favor.**

Can I have a napkin? » **Você me vê um guardanapo?**
Can you pass the salt, please? » **Me passa o sal, por favor.**
Could I get this to go? » **Você pode embrulhar pra viagem?**
Can I have the bill, please? » **Você me vê a conta, por favor?**
The meal was delicious. » **A refeição estava deliciosa.**
The service was excellent. » **O atendimento estava perfeito.**

**Problems**

Can I have another fork please? » **Você me vê um outro garfo, por favor?**
The food is cold. » **A comida está fria.**
I didn't order this. » **Eu não pedi isto.**
Is it going to be much longer? » **Vai demorar muito?**

## Key words

bill, check: **conta**
chef: **chefe de cozinha**
drink (noun): **bebida**
drink (verb): **beber**
eat: **comer**
food: **comida**
kitchen: **cozinha**
menu: **cardápio**
non-smoking section: **área de não fumantes**
reservation (for a table): **reserva**
smoking section: **área de fumantes**
table: **mesa**
terrace: **terraço**
tip: **gorjeta**
waiter: **garçom**

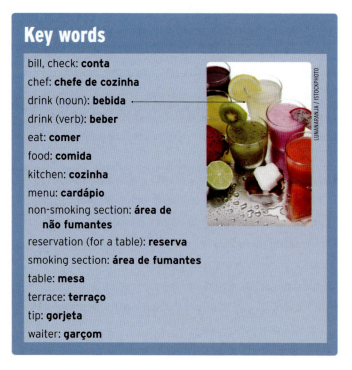

FOOD AND EATING OUT

## Meals

breakfast: **café da manhã**
dessert: **sobremesa**
dinner: **jantar**
entrée, starter, hors d'oeuvre: **entrada**
finger food, snacks, nibbles: **salgadinhos, petiscos**
lunch: **almoço**
snack, light meal: **refeição leve**
tea: **chá da tarde**

## At the table

bottle: **garrafa**
chair: **cadeira**
cup: **xícara**
fork: **garfo**
glass: **copo**
knife: **faca**
napkin: **guardanapo**
plate: **prato**
spoon: **colher**
straw: **canudo**
wine glass: **taça de vinho**

## Seafood

catfish: **bagre**
crab: **caranguejo**
crayfish: **pitu**
filet of sole: **filé de linguado**
fish: **peixe**
fish filet: **filé de peixe**
hake: **merluza**
lobster: **lagosta**
mussels: **mariscos, mexilhões**
needle fish: **agulha**
octopus: **polvo**
oyster: **ostra**
prawn, shrimp: **camarão**

89

**► Seafood**

salmon: **salmão**
salmon steak: **posta de salmão**
scallops: **vieiras**
seafood stew: **caldeirada de frutos do mar**
squid: **lula**
trout: **truta**
tuna: **atum**
weakfish: **pescada (common fish in Brazil with delicate, white flesh)**

## Meat and poultry

bacon: **toucinho**
breast (chicken): **peito**
chicken: **frango**
chicken thighs: **sobrecoxas**
chop: **costeleta**
drumsticks: **coxas**
duck: **pato**
gizzards: **moelas**
ground beef: **carne moída**
ham: **presunto**
kid: **cabrito**
lamb: **carneiro**
leg: **perna**
liver: **fígado**
pork: **carne de porco**
pork chops: **bisteca de porco**
ribs: **costela**
roast beef: **rosbife, carne assada**
roast chicken: **frango assado**
sausage: **linguiça**
steak: **bife, filé**
stewed chicken: **frango cozido**
strip or rib eye steak: **bife de contrafilé**
sucking pig: **leitão**
tripe: **bucho**
turkey: **peru**
veal: **vitela**
wing: **asa**

FOOD AND EATING OUT

# Fruit

**açaí** (The dark purple flesh of the açaí palm seed. It is used to make juice or served frozen in a bowl as a "slush".)
**acerola** (a small red tart Brazilian fruit used to make juice and ice cream)
apple: **maçã**
apricot: **damasco**
avocado: **abacate**
banana: **banana**
blackberry: **amora**
Brazil nut: **castanha do Pará**
**cajá** (a native Brazilian fruit from the north used for juices and ice cream)
cashew fruit: **caju**
cherimoya: **graviola**
cherry: **cereja**
coconut: **coco**
**cupuaçu** (a native Brazilian fruit from the north used for juices and ice cream)
custard apple, ata: **fruta do conde**
date: **tâmara**
fig: **figo**
grapes: **uva**
guava: **goiaba**
**jabuticaba** (a native Brazilian fruit eaten fresh)
kiwi fruit: **kiwi**
lemon: **limão-siciliano**
lime: **limão**
mandarin orange: **mandarina**
mango: **manga**
medlar: **nêspera**
melon: **melão**
orange: **laranja**
papaya: **mamão, papaya**
passion fruit: **maracujá**
peach: **pêssego**
pear: **pera**
pineapple: **abacaxi**
**pitanga** (a native Brazilian fruit with a very distinct flavour used to make juice and ice cream)

FRANCK OLIVIER GRONDIN / ISTOCKPHOTO

▶ Fruit

plum: **ameixa**
pomegranate: **romã**
prunes: **ameixas secas**
raisins: **uvas-passas**
raspberry: **framboesa**
star fruit: **carambola**
strawberry: **morango**
watermelon: **melancia**

## Vegetables

artichokes: **alcachofras**
beans: **feijão**
beet: **beterraba**
broccoli: **broccoli**
cabbage: **repolho**
carrot: **cenoura**
cauliflower: **couve-flor**
celery: **aipo**
chick peas: **grão-de-bico**
chili pepper: **pimenta**
corn: **milho**
cucumber: **pepino**
eggplant: **berinjela**
garlic: **alho**
green beans: **vagem**
lettuce: **alface**
manioc, cassava: **mandioca**
mushrooms: **cogumelos**
olives: **azeitonas**
onion: **cebola**
palm heart: **palmito**
palm oil: **dendê**
parsley: **salsinha**
peas: **ervilhas**
potato: **batata**
radish: **rabanete**
scallions: **cebolinha**
spinach: **espinafre**
squash: **abóbora**

FOOD AND EATING OUT

▶ Vegetables

string beans: **vagem**
sweet pepper: **pimentão**
tomato: **tomate**
turnip: **nabo**
vegetables: **verduras**
yam, sweet potato: **batata-doce**
zuccchini: **abobrinha**

## Drinks

beer: **cerveja**
black coffee: **cafezinho**
Brazilian national sugarcane rum: **cachaça**
coffee with hot milk: **café com leite**
draught beer: **chopp**
drink: **bebida**
dry (wine): **seco**
espresso: **espresso**
fruit juice: **suco**
mineral water: **água mineral**
mixed fruit juice made with milk: **vitamina**
pinga and lime cocktail: **caipirinha**
red wine: **vinho tinto**
softdrink, soda, pop: **refrigerante**
sparkling water: **água com gás**
sparkling white wine: **espumante**
tea: **chá**
white wine: **vinho branco**

## Cooking terms

baked: **assado**
barbecued: **feito na churrasqueira, na brasa**
boiled, steamed: **cozido**
breaded: **à milanesa**
chilled: **gelado**
chopped: **picado**
cook (verb): **cozinhar**
fresh: **fresco**
fried: **frito**

**▶ Cooking terms**

frozen: **congelado**
grilled: **grelhado**
medium (meat): **ao ponto**
medium rare: **entre ao ponto e malpassado**
peeled: **descascado**
rare: **malpassado**
raw: **cru**
roasted: **assado**
sautéed: **dourado**
scrambled: **mexido**
sliced: **fatiado**
well done (meat): **bem passado**

## Dairy products

butter: **manteiga**
cheese: **queijo**
cream cheese: **requeijão**
eggs: **ovos**
ice cream: **sorvete**
margarine: **margarina**
mild yellow cheese: **meia cura**
milk: **leite**
mozzarella: **muçarela**
parmesan (grated): **queijo parmesão, queijo ralado**
white cheese: **queijo branco, queijo minas**

## Herbs, spices and condiments

cinnamon: **canela**
cloves: **cravo**
coriander: **coentro**
garlic: **alho**
hot chili pepper: **pimenta**
jam: **geleia**
ketchup: **ketchup**
lime: **limão**
mayonaise: **maionese**
mustard: **mostarda**

FOOD AND EATING OUT

▶ Herbs, spices and condiments

olive oil: **azeite**
onion: **cebola**
oregano: **orégano**
parsley: **salsinha**
pepper (black): **pimenta-do-reino**
pickles: **picles**
rosemary: **alecrim**
sage: **sálvia**
salt: **sal**
sauce: **molho**
sugar: **açúcar**
thyme: **tomilho**
vinegar: **vinagre**

## Other main dishes and light meals

bread roll: **pão francês**
bread: **pão**
cheese burger with lettuce and tomatoes: **X-salada** (pronounced "sheess salada")
cheese platter: **prato de queijos**
cold cut platter: **prato de frios**
french fries: **batatas fritas**
ham and cheese sandwich: **misto-quente** (hot), **misto-frio** (cold)
hamburger: **hambúrguer**
omelette: **omelete**
pasta: **macarrão, massa**
pizza: **pizza**
rice and beans: **arroz e feijão**
salad: **salada**
sandwich: **sanduíche**
sliced bread: **pão de forma**
soup: **sopa**
steak: **bife**
toast: **torrada**
whole wheat bread: **pão integral**

# Going out and dating

**Nightlife**

Is there a nice bar near here? » **Tem algum bar legal por aqui?**

Is there a good restaurant near here? » **Tem algum restaurante bom por aqui?**

Is there a good place to dance near here? » **Tem algum lugar legal pra dançar por aqui?**

Is there a good place to listen to Brazilian music near here? » **Tem algum lugar legal pra ouvir música brasileira por aqui?**

Do you know a good place to meet new people? » **Você conhece algum lugar legal pra fazer novas amizades?**

Can you recommend a good place to go out at night? » **Você pode indicar um lugar legal pra sair à noite?**

Is there live music? » **Tem música ao vivo?**

Is there a cover charge? » **Tem couvert artístico?**

## GOING OUT AND DATING

What kind of music do they play? » **Que tipo de música eles tocam?**

Is there a dance floor? » **Tem pista de dança?**

I can't drink. I'm driving. » **Eu não posso beber. Estou dirigindo.**

OK, one for the road. » **Tá legal, a saideira.**

OK, just a drop. » **Tá legal, só um pouquinho.**

I'm drunk. » **Eu estou bêbado.**


### Meeting people

What's your name? » **Qual é o seu nome?**

Can I join you? » **Posso sentar aqui?**

My name is John. » **O meu nome é John.**

I'm from California. » **Eu sou da Califórnia.**

Would you like a drink? » **Você aceita uma bebida?**

Would you like to sit at our table? » **Você gostaria de sentar a nossa mesa?**

What's your phone number? » **Qual é o seu telefone?**

This is a nice place. » **Este é um lugar legal.**

I don't like it here. » **Eu não estou gostando daqui.**

Let's ask for the bill. » **Vamos pedir a conta.**

It's on me! » **É por minha conta!**

What's my share (of the bill)? » **Quanto eu devo?**


### Flirting

You look really nice. » **Você é muito bonita.** (said to a girl), **Você é muito bonito.** (said to a guy)

I like your dress. » **Gostei do seu vestido.**

You have a really nice smile. » **Você tem um sorriso lindo.**

Do you have a boyfriend? » **Você tem namorado?**

Do you have a girlfriend? » **Você tem namorada?**

Are you seeing anyone? » **Você está namorando?**

BRAZIL IN A NUTSHELL

Do you come here often? » **Você vem sempre aqui?**
Would you like to dance? » **Quer dançar?**
Would you like to go somewhere else? » **Você quer ir para um outro lugar?**
Can I call you some time? » **Posso ligar pra você?**
We should go out some time. » **A gente poderia sair um dia desses.**
Let's go to the movies? » **Vamos ao cinema?**
You're nice to talk to. » **É bom conversar com você.**
When can I see you again? » **Quando eu posso ver você de novo?**
I'd really like to see you again. » **Eu adoraria ver você de novo.**
You're nice. » **Você é legal.**
Do you want to come home with me? » **Você quer ir pra casa comigo?**

## Key words

bar: **bar**
boyfriend: **namorado**
condom: **camisinha**
dance floor: **pista de dance**
dance: **dançar**
date, go out with someone: **namorar**
discotheque: **discoteca**
fun: **diversão**
girlfriend: **namorada**
go out: **sair**
live music: **música ao vivo**
nightclub: **boate**
sex: **sexo**

## Drinks

beer: **cerveja**
coke: **Coca-cola**
drink (noun): **bebida**
dry martini: **dry martíni**
gin and tonic: **gim tônica**
ice: **gelo**
mineral water: **água mineral**
red wine: **vinho tinto**
rum and coke: **cuba-libre**
rum: **rum**
screwdriver: **vodca com suco de laranja**
shot: **dose**
slice of lime: **fatia de limão**
sparkling mineral water: **água com gás**
vodka: **vodca**
whisky: **uísque**
white wine: **vinho branco**

# Football / soccer

Rio's Maracanã stadium

## Questions and phrases

Where's the stadium? » **Onde fica o estádio?**

Where's the ticket office? » **Onde fica a bilheteria?**

What team do you support?, What team do you root for? » **Para que time você torce?**

When's the match between Brazil and England? » **Quando é o jogo do Brasil contra a Inglaterra?**

Do you have tickets for the match? » **Você tem ingressos para o jogo?**

Two tickets, numbered seats, please. » **Dois ingressos, nas numeradas, por favor.**

FOOTBALL / SOCCER

Four tickets, stand seats, please. » **Quatro ingressos, nas arquibancadas, por favor.**

Three tickets, bleachers, please. » **Três ingressos, nas arquibancadas, por favor.**

Two tickets, terraces, please. » **Dois ingressos, nas arquibancadas, por favor.**

What's the score? » **Qual é o placar?**

## Typical phrases

Still on! » **(A bola) não saiu!**

He missed the goal! » **Ele perdeu o gol!**

Come on! Pass the ball! » **Anda! Passa essa bola!**

Calm down! Take it easy! » **Calma! Devagar!**

Shoot! » **Chuta!**

Man on! » **Cuidado! Ladrão!**

He was brought down. » **Ele foi derrubado.**

He's acting! » **Ele está fingindo!**

It was a draw. » **O jogo empatou.**

He headed the ball towards the goal. » **Ele cabeceou para o gol.**

Great save! » **Grande defesa!**

Great move! » **Linda jogada!**

Hit the post! » **Na trave!**

The ref is blind! » **O juiz tá cego!**

That was close! » **Passou perto!**

What's the score? » **Quanto tá o jogo?**

It's one – nil. » **Tá um a zero.**

It's two – two. » **Tá dois a dois.**

It's a tie. » **Tá empatado.**

He was sent off. » **Ele foi expulso.**

The ref spotted a foul off the ball. » **O juiz marcou falta sem bola.**

He was booked. » **O juiz deu cartão amarelo pra ele.**

## Key words

5-aside: **5 de cada lado**
an own goal: **gol contra**
bench: **banco**
boo (verb): **vaiar**
booking (yellow card): **advertência (cartão amarelo)**
by-line: **linha de fundo**
centre forward: **centroavante**
changing rooms: **vestiários**
coach: **técnico**
corner: **escanteio**
cross-bar: **travessão**
crowds: **torcidas**
defence: **defesa**
defender: **zagueiro**
draw, tie: **empate**
dribble: **driblar**
dummy: **finta**
equalise: **empatar a partida**
equaliser: **gol de empate**
extra time, overtime: **prorrogação**
final whistle: **apito final**
first half: **primeiro tempo**
first leg: **jogo de ida**
football boots: **chuteiras**
forward: **atacante**
foul: **falta**
free kick: **cobrança de falta**
goal area: **pequena área**
goal keeper: **goleiro**
goal-kick: **tiro de meta**
half line: **meio-campo**
half-time: **intervalo**
injury-time: **acréscimos**

## FOOTBALL / SOCCER

kick-off: **pontapé inicial**
left winger: **ponteiro-esquerdo**
linesman: **bandeirinha, assistente**
manager: **técnico**
midfield: **meio de campo**
midfielder: **meio-campista**
net: **rede**
off side: **impedimento**
penalty box: **grande área**
penalty spot: **marca do pênalti**
pitch conditions: **condições do gramado**
play away: **jogar fora de casa**
play home: **jogar em casa**
rebound: **rebote**
referee, ref: **juiz**
re-match: **revanche**
right winger: **ponteiro-direito**
scissor kick: **bicicleta**
score (noun): **placar**
second half: **segundo tempo**
second leg: **jogo de volta**
sending off (red card): **expulsão (cartão vermelho)**
shinpads: **caneleiras**
side-line: **linha lateral**
sliding tackle: **carrinho**
stretch: **alongar**
striker: **atacante**
sweeper: **líbero**
tackle: **entrada**
terraces: **arquibancada**
throw-in: **arremesso lateral**
turnstile: **catraca**
wall: **barreira**
warm-up: **aquecimento**
wet: **molhado**

BRAZIL IN A NUTSHELL

# Olympic Games

**Olympic events and key words**

100 meter hurdle » **100 metros com barreiras**
2,500 meter steeplechase » **2.500 metros com barreiras**
champions » **campeões**
competitions » **provas**
decathlon » **decatlo**
field competition » **competição de campo**
finishing line » **linha de chegada**
hammer » **martelo**
high jump » **salto em altura**
hop, step and jump » **salto triplo**
hurdle » **provas com barreiras**
javelin throw » **arremesso de dardo**
lane » **raia, pista**
legs » **etapas**

104

OLYMPIC GAMES

long distance races » **corridas de fundo**

long jump » **salto em distância**

march » **marcha de 3.000 metros**

middle distance run » **corrida de meio-fundo**

pentathlon » **pentatlo**

pole vault » **salto com vara**

prizes » **prêmios**

qualifying rounds, qualifying heats, qualifying bouts » **eliminatórias**

race track » **pista de corrida**

referee » **juiz, árbitro**

relay » **revezamento**

run » **corrida**

score (noun) » **pontuação, placar**

shot put » **arremesso de peso**

sprinter » **velocista**

starting line » **linha de partida**

starting signal » **tiro de partida**

teams » **equipes**

weightlifting » **levantamento de peso**

JANIS LITAVNIEKS / ISTOCKPHOTO

## Gymnastics

apparatus » **aparelhos**

asymetric bars, uneven bars » **barras assimétricas**

beam » **trave**

floor exercise » **ginástica de solo**

horizontal bars » **barra fixa**

horse (box), vaulting horse » **cavalo de saltos**

long horse » **cavalo para saltos**

parallel bars » **barras paralelas**

rhythmic gymnastics » **ginástica rítmica, ginástica artística**

side horse, pommel horse » **cavalo de alças**
spring board, Reuther board » **trampolim**
swinging rings, stationary rings » **argolas**

## Combat sports

bantam weight » **peso-pena**
bout » **luta**
boxing » **pugilismo, boxe**
fly weight » **peso-mosca**
Graeco-Roman wrestling » **luta greco-romana**
heavy weight » **peso-pesado**
light heavyweith » **peso meio pesado**
light welterweight » **peso meio médio ligeiro, super ligeiro**
lightweight » **ligeiro**
middleweight » **peso médio**
welterweight » **peso meio-médio**
wrestling » **luta livre**

## Swimming

back stroke » **nado de costas**
breast stroke » **nado de peito**
butterfly stroke » **nado borboleta**
dive, diving » **salto, salto ornamental**
freestyle-crawl, front crawl » **nado livre**
lane » **raia**
medley relay » **competição mista com revezamento**
medley » **prova quarto estilos**
scissor kick » **tesoura**
swimming pool » **piscina**
turnover » **viradas**

OLYMPIC GAMES

## Water Polo

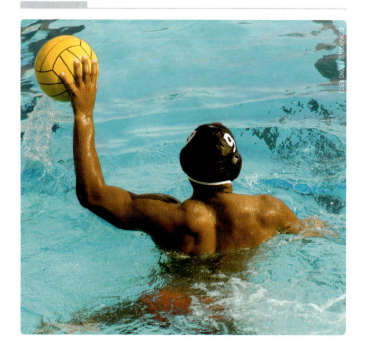

caps » **gorros**

cross bar » **baliza superior**

defense, back players » **defensores**

forward line players » **atacantes**

free throw » **tiro livre**

goal line » **linhas de gol**

goalkeepers » **goleiros**

goal-post » **balizas laterais**

halfline players » **médio**

minimum depth » **profundidade mínima**

penalty throw » **pênalti, tiro livre de 4 metros**

reserve players » **jogadores reservas**

team players » **jogadores titulares**

timekeepers » **cronometristas**

## Canoeing

bow » **proa**

canoe doubles, doublescull » **canoa a dois**

conoe single » **canoa individual**

cox » **timoneiro**

coxless pair » **sem timoneiro**

foursome » **a quatro**

kayak doubles » **caiaque a dois**

kayak single » **caiaque individual**

rowing, oar, paddle » **remo, pá**

stern » **popa**

with skipper » **com patrão**

yachting » **iatismo**

## Diving

armstand dive » **salto em equilíbrio**

backward dive » **salto de costas**

diver » **saltador**

diving tower » **torre de saltos**

diving » **saltos ornamentais**

entry » **entrada**

flight » **voo**

forward dive » **salto de frente**

header » **esticado**

inward dive » **salto para dentro**

pike diver, jack-knife » **carpado**

reverse dive » **salto invertido**

twist dive » **saca-rolhas**

## Ball and racket games

badminton » **peteca com raquete**
basketball » **basquete**
handball » **handebol**
soccer » **futebol**
table tennis » **tênis de mesa**
tennis » **tênis**
volleyball » **voleibol**

## Volleyball

attack » **ataque**
block » **bloqueio**
captain » **capitão**
central line » **linha central**
defense player » **jogador de defesa**
end line » **linha de fundo**
foul » **falta**
hit » **golpear, cortar**
linesman » **juiz de linha**
net » **rede**

opponent team » **equipe adversária**
opponent » **adversário**
referee » **primeiro árbitro**
rotation movement » **movimento de rotação**
rotation system » **sistema rotativo**
rules » **regras**
service » **saque**
serving area » **área de saque**
sets » **parciais**
side lines » **linhas laterais**
spiking » **cortada**
spiking line » **linha de ataque**
substitution » **substituição**
to carry » **conduzir**
to hold » **segurar**
umpire » **segundo árbitro**

## Basketball

back board » **tabela**
basket » **cesta**
counter attack » **contra-ataque**
cutting, screening » **corta-luz**
defense » **defesa**
forward » **armador**
free throw line » **linha de lance livre**
free throw » **lance livre**
held ball » **bola presa**
jump ball » **bola ao alto**
man to man defense » **marcação homem a homem**
out of bound ball » **bola morta**
pass » **passe**

personal foul » **falta pessoal**

pivot » **pivô**

possession of the ball » **posse de bola**

referee » **juiz**

rim, hoop » **aro**

to bounce » **quicar**

to retreat, to drawback » **esquivar**

to slam dunk » **enterrar**

to throw, to toss, to shoot » **arremessar**

umpire » **fiscal**

zone defense » **marcação por zona**

## Tennis

baseline » **linha de fundo**

linesman » **fiscal de linha**

net » **rede**

net judge » **fiscal de rede**

service » **saque**

smash » **cortada**

umpire » **juiz**

## Archery

arrow » **flecha**
bow » **arco**

## Cycling

against watch 100 km time trial » **100 quilômetros contra o relógio**
American race » **corrida americana**
cyclist » **ciclista**
free wheel » **roda livre**
front traction » **tração dianteira**
gear » **engrenagem, marcha**
individual pursuit » **perseguição individual**
individual road race » **corrida individual de estrada**
pedal » **pedal**
scratch speed » **velocidade de "scratch"**
"tandem speed" » **velocidade de "tandem"**
"team pursuit" » **perseguição por equipe**
velodrome » **velódromo**

## Fencing

épée team » **espada por equipe**
foil team » **florete por equipe**
individual épée » **espada individual**
individual sabre » **sabre individual**
sabre team » **sabre por equipe**

## Horsemanship / horse riding

individual dressage » **adestramento individual**
individual show jumping » **salto com obstáculos individual**
team dressage » **adestramento em equipe**
team show jumping » **salto em equipe**

## Shooting

air pistol » **pistola de ar comprimido**
air riffle » **carabina de ar comprimido**
free pistol » **pistola livre**
free riffle (three positions) » **carabina livre (três posições)**
running target » **alvo móvel**
small-bore riffle (lying) » **carabina de pequeno calibre (deitado)**
small-bore riffle (three positions) » **carabina de pequeno calibre (3 posições)**

# Glossary of useful language

## Special occasions

Have a nice trip. » **Boa viagem.**

Bon appetite. » **Bom apetite.**

Happy birthday! » **Feliz aniversário!**

Happy Easter! » **Feliz Páscoa!**

Happy new year! » **Feliz ano-novo!**

Merry Christmas! » **Feliz Natal!**

Congratulations! » **Parabéns!**

## Cardinal numbers

1 » **um, uma**

2 » **dois, duas**

3 » **três**

4 » **quatro**

5 » **cinco**

6 » **seis**

7 » **sete**

8 » **oito**

9 » **nove**

10 » **dez**

11 » **onze**

12 » **doze**

# GLOSSARY OF USEFUL LANGUAGE

13 » **treze**

14 » **quatorze/ catorze**

15 » **quinze**

16 » **dezesseis**

17 » **dezessete**

18 » **dezoito**

19 » **dezenove**

20 » **vinte**

21 » **vinte e um**

22 » **vinte e dois**

23 » **vinte e três**

29 » **vinte e nove**

30 » **trinta**

40 » **quarenta**

50 » **cinquenta**

60 » **sessenta**

70 » **setenta**

80 » **oitenta**

90 » **noventa**

100 » **cem**

101 » **cento e um**

102 » **cento e dois**

125 » **cento e vinte e cinco**

200 » **duzentos**

300 » **trezentos**

400 » **quatrocentos**

500 » **quinhentos**

600 » **seiscentos**

700 » **setecentos**

800 » **oitocentos**

900 » **novecentos**

1,000 » **mil**

1,020 » **mil e vinte**

1,345 » **mil, trezentos e quarenta e cinco**

2,000 » **dois mil**

3,000 » **três mil**

1,000,000 » **um milhão**

2,000,000 » **dois milhões**

4,456,739 » **quatro milhões, quatrocentos e cinquenta e seis mil, setecentos e trinta e nove**

1,000,000,000 » **um bilhão**

## Ordinal numbers

1st first » **primeiro**

2nd second » **segundo**

3rd third » **terceiro**

4th fourth » **quarto**

5th fifth » **quinto**

6th sixth » **sexto**

7th seventh » **sétimo**

8th eighth » **oitavo**

9th ninth » **nono**

10th tenth » **décimo**

11th eleventh » **décimo primeiro**

12th twelfth » **décimo segundo**

13th thirteenth » **décimo terceiro**

14th fourteenth » **décimo quarto**

15th fifteenth » **décimo quinto**

16th sixteenth » **décimo sexto**

17th seventh » **décimo sétimo**

18th eighteenth » **décimo oitavo**

19th nineteenth » **décimo nono**

20th twentieth » **vigésimo**

21st twenty-first » **vigésimo primeiro**

22nd twenty-second » **vigésimo segundo**

30th thirtieth » **trigésimo**

40th fortieth » **quadragésimo**

50th fiftieth » **quinquagésimo**

100th hundredth » **centésimo**

101st one hundred and first » **centésimo primeiro**

1000th thousandth » **milésimo**

## Measurements

centimeter » **centímetro**

feet » **pés**

inch » **polegada**

kilometer » **quilômetro**

meter » **metro**

mile » **milha**

milimeter » **milímetro**

yard » **jarda**

## Dimensions

height » **altura**

depth » **profundidade**

length » **comprimento**

width » **largura**

## Percents

10% ten percent » **dez por cento**

20% twenty percent » **vinte por cento**

100% one hundred per cent » **cem por cento**

## Fractions

½ – one half » **meio**

¼ – one fourth » **um quarto**

¾ – three fourths » **três quartos**

0.5 – zero point five » **0,5 zero vírgula cinco**

3.4 – three point four » **3,4 três vírgula quatro**

## Days of the week

Monday » **segunda-feira, segunda**

Tuesday » **terça-feira, terça**

Wednesday » **quarta-feira, quarta**

Thursday » **quinta-feira, quinta**

Friday » **sexta-feira, sexta**

Saturday » **sábado**

Sunday » **domingo**

## Months of the year

January » **janeiro**

February » **fevereiro**

March » **março**

April » **abril**

May » **maio**

June » **junho**

July » **julho**

August » **agosto**

September » **setembro**

October » **outubro**

November » **novembro**

December » **dezembro**

GLOSSARY OF USEFUL LANGUAGE

## The time

Do you have the time, please? » **Você tem horas, por favor?**

What time is it please? » **Que horas são, por favor?**

It's two o'clock. » **São duas horas.**

It's (a) quarter past seven. » **São sete e quinze.**

It's half past three. » **São três e meia.**

It's ten to eight. » **São dez para as oito.**

## Colors

beige » **bege**

black » **preto**

blue » **azul**

brown » **marrom**

dark green » **verde escuro**

gray » **cinza**

green » **verde**

light blue » **azul-claro**

orange » **laranja**

pink » **rosa**

purple » **roxo**

red » **vermelho**

white » **branco**

yellow » **amarelo**

## Asking questions

Where? » **Onde?**

When? » **Quando?**

At what time? » **A que horas?**

To where? » **Aonde?, Para onde?**

BRAZIL IN A NUTSHELL

With whom? » **Com quem?**

From where? » **De onde?**

What? » **O quê?, Quê?**

Who? » **Quem?**

How? » **Como?**

When? » **Quando?**

Whose? » **De quem?**

Where? » **Onde?**

Why? » **Por quê?**

Why not? » **Por que não?**

To whom? » **Para quem?**

Which one? » **Qual?**

What kind? » **Que tipo?**

How much? » **Quanto?**

How much is it? » **Quanto é?**

How many? » **Quantos?**

About whom? » **Sobre quem?**

## Useful words and phrases

a little » **um pouco**

a lot » **muito, bastante**

and » **e**

another » **outro(a)**

bad » **ruim**

big » **grande**

but » **mas**

Cheers! » **Saúde!**

closed » **fechado**

Come in. » **Entre.**

Congratulations! » **Parabéns!**

entrance » **entrada**

## GLOSSARY OF USEFUL LANGUAGE

everything » **tudo**

exit » **saída**

for » **para**

get out » **saia**

good » **bom**

Good luck! » **Boa sorte!**

here » **aqui**

I feel ill. » **Eu estou me sentindo mal.**

I want to see a doctor. » **Eu preciso de um médico.**

I'll phone you. » **Eu te ligo.**

I'm hungry. » **Eu estou com fome.**

I'm thirsty. » **Eu estou com sede.**

I'm tired. » **Estou cansado(a).**

It's boring. » **É chato.**

It's cold. » **Está frio.**

It's great! » **Ótimo!**

It's hot. » **Está quente.**

It's near here. » **Fica aqui perto.**

It's too far away. » **Fica muito longe.**

later » **depois, mais tarde**

left » **esquerdo(a)**

less » **menos**

more » **mais**

nothing » **nada**

now » **agora**

open » **aberto**

pull » **puxe**

push » **empurre**

quickly » **rápido**

right » **direito(a)**

Sit down. » **Sente-se.**

slow down » **devagar**

slowly » **devagar**

small » **pequeno**

something » **alguma coisa**

sometimes » **às vezes**

stop » **pare**

straight on » **direto**

that » **esse, aquele (masc.), essa, aquela (fem.)**

this » **este (masc.), esta (fem.)**

today » **hoje**

tomorrow » **amanhã**

## Time expressions

a bit later » **pouco tempo depois**

a couple of days ago » **alguns dias atrás**

a long time ago » **há muito tempo**

after » **depois**

always » **sempre**

at night » **à noite**

before » **antes**

early » **cedo**

early in the morning » **bem cedinho**

every now and then » **de vez em quando**

every other day » **dia sim, dia não**

in a couple of weeks » **daqui a duas semanas**

in autumn; in fall » **no outono**

in spring » **na primavera**

in summer » **no verão**

in the afternoon » **à tarde**

in the evening » **à noite**

in the morning » **de manhã**

## GLOSSARY OF USEFUL LANGUAGE

in winter » no inverno

last month » mês passado

last night » ontem à noite

last Saturday » sábado passado

last week » semana passada

last year » no ano passado

late » tarde

later » mais tarde

never » nunca

next Sunday » domingo que vem

next time » na próxima vez

next week » semana que vem

now » agora

nowadays » hoje em dia

on Christmas Eve » na véspera do Natal

ontem » yesterday

some days before » poucos dias antes

some years ago » alguns anos atrás

sometimes » às vezes

the day after tomorrow » depois de amanhã

the day before yesterday » anteontem

this morning » hoje de manhã

three years ago » três anos atrás

today » hoje

tomorrow » amanhã

tomorrow morning » amanhã de manhã

tonight » hoje à noite

too late » tarde demais

two weeks ago » semana retrasada

very late » muito tarde

## General interactive phrases

After you! » **Você primeiro!**

All set? » **Tudo pronto?**

All the best! » **Tudo de bom!**

Alone at last! » **Enfim, sós!**

And how! » **E como!**

And that's all! » **E ponto final!**

Anybody home? » **Tem alguém em casa?**

Are you OK? » **Você está bem?**

As you wish. » **Como você quiser.**

Big deal! » **Grande coisa!**

Bless you! (sneezing) » **Saúde!**

Calm down! » **Calma!**

Cheer up! » **Ânimo!**

Coming! » **Já estou indo!**

Count me in. » **Conte comigo.**

Count me out. » **Eu estou fora.**

Cross my heart! » **Juro por Deus!**

Cut it out! » **Pare com isso!**

Damn (it)! » **Droga!**

Dinner is served. » **O jantar está servido.**

Don't I know it? » **E você acha que eu não sei?**

Don't mention it. » **Não há de quê.**

Don't you dare! » **Não se atreva!**

Enjoy yourself. » **Divirta-se.**

For heaven's sake! » **Pelo amor de Deus!**

Forget it! » **Deixa pra lá!**

Get lost! » **Cai fora!**

Get well soon. » **Estimo as melhoras.**

Go for it! » **Manda bala!**

God only knows! » **Só Deus sabe!**

## GLOSSARY OF USEFUL LANGUAGE

Guess what? » **Adivinha só!**

Hands off! » **Tira as mãos daí!**

Have a good time! » **Divirta-se!**

Have a nice day! » **Tenha um bom dia!**

Have a good trip! » **Boa viagem!**

Have fun! » **Divirta-se!**

Have you heard the latest? » **Já sabe da última?**

Heads or tails? » **Cara ou coroa?**

Heaven forbid! » **Deus me livre!**

Help yourself! » **Sirva-se!**

Help! » **Socorro!**

Here you are! » **Aqui está!**

Hold your horses! » **Calma aí!**

How dare you? » **Como você ousa?**

How have you been? » **Como tem passado?**

Hurry up! » **Anda logo!**

I beg your pardon? » **Poderia repetir, por favor?**

I couldn't care less! » **Eu não dou a mínima!**

I didn't mean to hurt you. » **Eu não quis magoá-la.**

I hope I'm not disturbing you. » **Espero não estar incomodando.**

I love you. » **Te amo.**

I mean it! » **Estou falando sério!**

I miss you. » **Estou com saudades.**

I see! » **Entendo!, Sei!**

I'd love to... » **Eu adoraria...**

I'll be right back. » **Volto já.**

I'll get it. (the door or phone) » **Eu atendo.**

I'm sorry to hear that. » **Sinto muito.**

It never rains, but it pours. » **Desgraça pouca é bobagem.**

It's not what you think! » **Não é o que você está pensando!**

It's on me! » **É por minha conta!**

# BRAZIL IN A NUTSHELL

It's up to you. » **Fica a seu critério.**

Keep the change. » **Fique com o troco.**

Knock on wood! » **Isola!**

Ladies first! » **As damas primeiro!**

Listen to this! » **Escuta essa!**

Look who's here! » **Olha quem está aqui!**

Make yourself at home. » **Fique à vontade.**

May I come in? » **Posso entrar?**

May I have your attention, please? » **Atenção, por favor!**

Mind your own business! » **Isso não é da sua conta!**

Mum's the word! » **Bico calado!**

My pleasure! » **O prazer é meu!**

My sympathy. » **Meus pêsames.**

Nice talking to you. » **Foi bom falar com você.**

No comment! » **Sem comentário!**

No kidding! » **Verdade?**

No way! » **Sem chance!**

Nothing doing! » **Nada feito!**

Now what? » **E agora?**

Says who? » **Quem disse?**

Scram! » **Desapareça!**

Serves you right! » **Bem feito!**

Shame on you! » **Que vergonha!**

Shut up! » **Cala a boca!**

Sleep tight. » **Durma bem.**

So what? » **E daí?**

Sweet dreams! » **Sonhe com os anjos!**

Take your time. » **Não tenha pressa.**

That's all! » **É isso aí!**

That's very nice of you. » **É muita gentileza sua.**

The same to you. » **Pra você também.**

This way, please. » **Por aqui, por favor.**

# GLOSSARY OF USEFUL LANGUAGE

Time's up. » **Tempo acabou.**

Wait a minute! » **Espera aí!**

Wait and see! » **Espere só para ver!**

Wanna bet? » **Quer apostar?**

Watch out! » **Cuidado!**

Watch your step. » **Cuidado com o degrau.**

What a pity! » **Que pena!**

What a shame! » **Que pena!**

What are you doing here? » **O que você está fazendo aqui?**

Who do you think you're talking to? » **Com quem você pensa que está falando?**

Will you marry me? » **Quer casar comigo?**

You bet! » **Pode apostar!**

You can't miss it! » **Não tem como errar!**

You don't say! » **Não diga!**

You said it! » **Você disse tudo!**

You tell 'em! » **Dá-lhe!**

You're my guest. » **Você é o meu convidado.**

Your tough luck! » **Azar o seu!**

BRAZIL IN A NUTSHELL

## Appendix

# Brazilian Portuguese pronunciation

For the most part, Brazilian Portuguese is pronounced the way it's spelled. This should bring a sigh of relief to the lips of any English speaker who is used to things being spelled one way and pronounced another way altogether. However, there are a few things that English-speaking people have to keep in mind when speaking in Portuguese:

### Stresses in Brazilian Portuguese

As a general rule, any accent in a Portuguese word marks the stressed syllable. Capital letters represent the stressed syllables in the example words below.

# Vowels in Brazilian Portuguese

**NON-NASAL VOWELS**

Usually somewhere between the "**a**" sound of "**cat**" and that of "**farm**".
**EXAMPLES** » CArro (car), lar (home).

Two main pronunciations:

At the beginning or in the middle of a word it sounds like "**e**" in "**bet**".
**EXAMPLES** » FESta (party), MÉdico (doctor).

At the end of a word "**e**" sounds like the "**y**" in "**pretty**".
**EXAMPLES** » GENte (people), alFAce (lettuce).

Always sounds like an "**ee**" sound like the "**i**" in "**police**".
**EXAMPLES** » VISto (visa).

Three possible pronunciations:

At the beginning or in the middle of a word it sounds like the "**o**" in "**dog**" or like the "**o**" in "**go**".
**EXAMPLES** » MOla (spring), PObre (poor), show (show), GLObo (globe).

At the end of a word "**o**" sounds like the "**oo**" in "**book**".
**EXAMPLES** » esTAdo (state), obriGAdo (thank you).

Always pronounced like "**oo**" as in "**book**".
**EXAMPLES** » BLUsa (blouse).

## NASAL VOWELS

Nasal vowels are a challenge and usually difficult for English speakers to reproduce.

-ã and -am or -an after a consonant sound like a nasal "**a**".
EXAMPLES » sã (sane), TAMpa (cap),
SANto (saint), SAMba (samba).

-ão or -am at the end of a word have a nasal "**ow**" sound.
EXAMPLES » chão (floor), canÇÃO (song),
mão (hand), CANtam (they sing).

-em or -en after a consonant have a nasalized "**e**" sound.
EXAMPLES » TEMpo (time), QUENte (hot).

-em or -ens at the end of a word have a nasalized "**ehn**" sound.
EXAMPLES » trem (train), paSSAgens (tickets).

-im or -in at the end of a word or after
a consonant have a nasal "**ee**" sound.
EXAMPLES » sim (yes), interiOR (countryside).

-om or -on at the end of a word or after
a consonant have a nasal "**o**" sound.
EXAMPLES » bom (good), tom (tone), CONtra (against).

-um or -un at the end of a word or after
a consonant have a nasal "**u**" sound.
EXAMPLES » um (one), JUNto (together).

-ãe has a nasal "**ai**" sound.
EXAMPLES » mãe (mother), pães (bread).

-õe has a nasal "**oin**" sound.
EXAMPLES » ações (actions), manSÕES (mansions).

Note that most words ending in "-ão"
form their plural by adding an "**ões**" at the end.

APPENDIX

# Consonants in Brazilian Portuguese

Most of them are straightforward and pronounced as in English. There are a few exceptions shown below.

**C**

Usually pronounced hard as in "**cap**".
EXAMPLES » cantar (sing).
When followed by "**i**" or "**e**" it's
pronounced like an "**s**", as in "**city**".
EXAMPLES » ciNEma (movie theater), CEna (scene).
It's also pronounced as an "**s**" whenever
it's written with a cedilla accent.
EXAMPLES » ação (action), aÇOUgue (butcher's).

**CH**

Pronounced like an English "**sh**".
EXAMPLES » CHAve (key), CHEIro (smell).

**D**

Pronounced as in English or at times palatized to sound
like "**dj**" whenever it comes before an "**i**" or final "**e**".
EXAMPLES » dia (day), de (of).

**G**

Hard like in English as in "**good**".
EXAMPLES » GAto (cat), GRANde (big).
Before "**e**" or "**i**" it's pronounced like the "**s**"
in English word "**vision**".
EXAMPLES » GENte (people), giGANte (giant).

**H**

Always silent.
EXAMPLES » HOmem (man), HOra (hour).

**J**

Pronounced like the "**s**" in English word "**vision**" or "**measure**".
EXAMPLES » JAto (jet), jorNAL (newspaper).

### BRAZIL IN A NUTSHELL

### L

Usually as in English. At the end of a word
it sounds a bit like a "**w**".
EXAMPLES » hoTEL (hotel), mal (bad).
When followed by "**h**", it's pronounced
"**ly**" as in the English word "**million**".
EXAMPLES » MIlho (corn), FIlha (daughter).

### N

As in English. When it's followed by "**h**"
it becomes "**nhyo**" or "**nhya**".
EXAMPLES » NInho (nest), maNHÃ (morning).

### Q

Always followed by "**u**" and is
pronounced either "**k**" or "**kw**".
EXAMPLES » queRIda (darling), freQUENte (frequent).

### R

Usually as in English. At the beginning of
a word it's pronounced like an English "**h**".
EXAMPLES » rua (street), RAto (rat).

### RR

Always pronounced like an English "**h**".
EXAMPLES » gaRRAfa (bottle), caCHOrro (dog).

### S

Usually pronounced like an English "**s**".
EXAMPLES » saco (bag), sapato (shoe).
In some parts of Brazil (Rio for example)
it's pronounced like an English "**sh**" when it becomes
before a consonant and at the end of a word.
EXAMPLES » isQUEIro (lighter), esCRAvo (slave), caVAlos (horses).

### T

Usually as in English, but it changes
to "**chee**" before "**i**" and final "**e**".
EXAMPLES » atiRAR (shoot), MORte (death).

APPENDIX

Like an English "**sh**" at the beginning of a word and elsewhere like an English "**x**" or "**z**".
EXAMPLES » xaDREZ (chess), exerCÍcio (exercise).

## Key words

accent: **sotaque**
hear: **escutar**
language: **língua, linguagem**
letter: **letra**
listen: **ouvir, escutar**
pronunciation: **pronúncia**
sound: **som**
speak: **falar**
talk: **conversar, falar**
word: **palavra**

# Useful phone numbers and websites

## EMERGENCY SERVICES AND THEIR TELEPHONE NUMBERS

Ambulance » **Ambulância 192**

Anonymous Crime Reporting » **Disque Denúncia 181**

Civil Defence Department » **Defesa Civil 199**

Civil Police » **Polícia Civil 197**

Emergency Services within the Mercosul » **Serviços de Emergência no Âmbito do Mercosul 128**

Federal Highway Police » **Polícia Rodoviária Federal 191**

Federal Police » **Polícia Federal 194**

Fire department » **Corpo de Bombeiros 193**

Military Police » **Polícia Militar 190**

Police Departments that Attend Women » **Delegacias Especializadas de Atendimento à Mulher 180**

State Highway Police » **Polícia Rodoviária Estadual 198**

APPENDIX

## SPECIAL SERVICES

Brazilian Ministry of Tourism » **(61) 3429-7729**

Infraero (the government transportation agency that controls airports in Brazil and where you can check flight times and details anywhere in Brazil) » **http://www.infraero.gov.br/**

International Telephone Operator » **101**

Telephone Directory Information » **102**

## GENERAL INFORMATION ABOUT BRAZIL

BBC • Brazil country profile »
**http://news.bbc.co.uk/2/hi/europe/country_profiles/1227110.stm**

Brazilian Institute of Geography and Statistics (IBGE) »
**http://www.ibge.gov.br/home/**

Brazilian Ministry of Tourism »
**http://www.turismo.gov.br/turismo/home.html**

United Nations • data on Brazil »
**http://data.un.org/CountryProfile.aspx?crName=BRAZIL**

Wikipedia • Brazil »
**http://en.wikipedia.org/wiki/Brazil**

Wikitravel • Brazil »
**http://wikitravel.org/en/Brazil**

World Health Organization / Health topics »
**http://www.who.int/topics/en/**

Este livro foi impresso em fevereiro de 2012
pela Yangraf Gráfica e Editora Ltda.,
sobre papel couchê brilho 90g/m².